The Bug Book

for Gardeners

by

Theo Gedge

Kenneth Mason Publications Limited

The Bug Book for Gardeners

© Kenneth Mason Publications Limited
The Book Barn, Westbourne, Hampshire, PO10 8RS, UK   +44 (0)1243 377977
Text copyright © Theo Gedge 2007
A catalogue record for this title is available from the British Library.

Printed in Italy by Grafica Veneta SpA

ISBN 978-0-85937-405-7

Acknowledgements
The author and publishers are very grateful to the following
for the use of their photographic material.

Robert Brown
Solomon's seal sawfly larvae p14, Magpie moth caterpillar p27,
Banded demoiselle p64, Common wasp p65

NHPA
Leatherjacket p11, Sawfly p13, Black ant p20, Large white butterfly caterpillar p21,
Large white butterfly eggs p21, Lily beetle p28, Colorado beetle p30,
Cockchafer p31, Click beetle p32, Wireworm p32, Vine weevil p35, Vine weevil
larvae p36, Earwigs p38, Black bean aphid p40, Rose aphid p40, Red ant and
aphids p41, Plum aphids p42, Adult gladiolus thrip p43, Froghopper p44,
Common green capsid p45, Leafhopper p46, Mealybugs p47, Whitefly p49,
Woodlouse p51, Snake millipede p52, Black millipede p53, Garden snail p55,
Spider mites p59, Ladybird eating black aphids p62, Ladybird larva p62,
Hoverfly p63, Green lacewing larvae p63, Green lacewing p63, Bumble bee p64,
Honey bee p65, Centipede p67, Potter wasp p66

FLPA
Cabbage root fly larvae p15, Carrot fly larva in carrot p16, Sciarid fly p18,
Pear sucker psyllid p19, Small white butterfly caterpillars p22,
Looper caterpillar of angle shades moth p23, Common cutworm p24,
Ghost swift moth caterpillar p25, Pea moth caterpillar p25,
Codling moth caterpillar p26, Larvae of lily beetle p29, Cockchafer larva p31,
Flea beetle p33, Flea beetle damage to radish p33, Raspberry beetle larva p34,
Strawberry seed beetle p35, Pea & bean weevil damage p37, Thrip damage p44,
Leafhopper nymphs p46, Leafhopper damage p46, Scale insects p47,
Immature springtail p54, Grey field slug p56

The Bug Book for Gardeners

Contents

About the Author

With a lifelong passion for gardening and after many years experience of advisory work in both horticultural and agricultural crop protection, Theo Gedge is well qualified to share his knowledge of plant pests, their identification and how to control them. A keen conservationist and advocate of natural pest control methods, he strongly believes in the urgent need to reduce the pollution of our environment and in the protection of our natural heritage.

Qualified as an official seed crop inspector, he worked for many years for an international crop protection company advising farmers, market growers and gardeners on soil health, fertility, plant health, plant diseases and pest control. He has run his own livestock farm, a market garden and a successful bedding plant nursery.

Despite being a conservationist he is fully aware that from time to time plant protection products have to be used in our gardens. If spraying is necessary, then only the safest and most effective products are suggested in this book. Theo lives with his wife in Sussex where he is a head gardener and horticultural advisor to a Downland country estate.

Introduction

It is essential to know which of the many insects in our gardens are harmless and which are pests. Whilst this book is not intended to be fully comprehensive it gives a selection of the more common creatures we come across and what to do about them. Whether as occasional, or experienced, gardeners we are often confronted with the problem of plant damage, either by the weather, plant diseases or by pests attacking and spoiling everything in the garden.

The title of this book reflects the unpleasant fact that some creatures really do 'bug' the gardener and its content tries to cover many of the more common pests. It also offers some guidance as to identifying them and what to do if they need to be controlled.

Many of these pests are insects, but not all insects are pests. Many insects are useful in a number of ways, so included in this book is a small section devoted to some of the more helpful insects that might be encountered. Good gardeners appreciate that gardens are a whole world in microcosm with natural processes and evolution taking place all the time, often despite our efforts to exercise control over them. All the creatures we encounter, good and bad, have every right to be there so we must choose, for the sake of our plants, if it is imperative to control them or to leave them to get on with their lives.

The book covers some of the chemical pest controls available to the domestic gardener along with some of the latest biological products available to the domestic market. Also covered are some more traditional methods of control, as valid today as they were then, that our forbears used hundreds of years ago before today's chemicals were discovered.

How to use this book

When faced with damage to our plants, the questions are 'What has caused this damage?' 'Can it be rectified?' and 'Can we stop the damage occurring again?'

Correct identification of the pest causing the damage is the essential starting point. Once this is properly established the action taken to eradicate the pest can be entirely appropriate. It is useless to spend time, effort and money in spraying an aphicide onto a plant suffering from red spider mite infestation or to put slug pellets around the strawberries when the real culprits are the blackbirds.

The book covers the types of damage that pests can inflict upon plants. Some damage is unmistakable, even to an untrained eye, and the pest easily identified whilst some can be trickier as a number of different pests can inflict very similar damage. Of course identification is much easier if the pest is visible on the plant, it being a simple matter to go through the photographs in this book to identify it.

Pest Groups

Insects and their larvae attack plants to feed themselves in two ways. Some are 'biters and chewers', feeding on leaves, stems, roots and flowers, while others are 'suckers', piercing the plant tissue and feeding solely on the plant sap. Some, including most of the sap feeders, content themselves by staying on the outside of their food plant. Others tunnel into the plant stems and roots, keeping safely hidden away as they feed on the plant tissue.

Many insects are most damaging to our plants when they are in the immature larval state, this is particularly so in the case of butterflies and moths. The adults do little if any damage but their young, the caterpillars, are some of the most destructive pests the gardener has to contend with. This however is not the case with other groups of insects. Many beetles and flies are just as damaging to our plants in the adult stage as they are when they are in the young larval state.

Not all garden pests are insects of course, millipedes, woodlice, slugs and snails, and others, belong to different animal orders such as crustacea and molluscs. The damaging red spider mite and other small mites do not belong to the insect order. They have eight legs, whereas insects have only six. It should also be remembered that although a number of sap sucking insects are described as 'true bugs', they still belong to the insect order.

The 5 Pest Groups

1. Flies

2. Butterflies & moths

3. Beetles

4. True bugs

5. Spider mites, millipedes, eelworms, woodlice and others, such as mammals and birds

Groups 1 to 4 are all insect pests.

All in Group 5 belong to other animal orders.

Pest Group 1

Two winged, or true flies

Houseflies, Gnats, Mosquitoes, Midges, Crane flies (Daddy long legs), Cabbage rootfly, Carrot fly, Sciarid flies and Leaf miner flies.

The larvae of this group are without legs, and are collectively known as maggots. Many are very damaging to plants.

Other flies

These flies usually have two pairs of wings, and include sawflies, wasps, bees and ants. Sawflies in particular are very damaging pests in the larval state, resembling the caterpillars of butterflies. Unlike caterpillars sawfly larvae have at least six pairs of stumpy prolegs, whereas caterpillars have never more than five . Adult sawflies do little harm as they feed mainly on flower and tree pollen.

Pest Group 2

Butterflies and moths

No damage is caused in the garden by adult butterflies and moths but their young larvae, the caterpillars, are often very destructive pests. Caterpillars have three pairs of true legs as well as up to five fleshy prolegs to the rear of the body. They are easily distinguished from the fly maggots which are legless.

Pest Group 3

Beetles, including the earwig

This is the largest insect order and contains many serious garden pests. Both larvae and adults are often equally damaging. The larvae vary, some being legless maggots while others have hard, well developed bodies and strong legs. Some beetles such as the ladybird are valuable allies in the garden as they devour pests such as aphids and mites.

Pest Group 4

The true bugs

This is a vast and diverse group of insects which includes aphids, leaf hoppers, capsids, frog hoppers, mealy bugs, scale insects, suckers and whitefly. All are sap feeders and many carry virus diseases from plant to plant as well as seriously debilitating the host plant by their feeding.

Pest Group 5

Woodlice
These are terrestial crustaceans that live in damp and humid conditions, often eating the margins of leaves and flowers.

Millipedes
Segmented arthropods that live in the soil. They have two pairs of legs per segment and are not to be confused with centipedes which are useful carnivorous predators that have only one pair per segment and are usually brightly coloured. Millipedes feed on decaying matter in the soil, plant roots and tubers such as dahlias and potatoes.

Springtails
These are wingless arthropods that are related to true insects and cause similar damage to that of the flea beetle. In mid-summer they are often seen in great numbers in the garden.

Symphylids
Rarely a problem in the garden, but can cause some damage if tomatoes are regularly grown in greenhouse borders in a chalky or limy soil. Regular, thorough border soil cultivation prevents the build up of symphylid populations.

Slugs and Snails
Both these molluscs are very harmful in the garden and can seriously damage plants. Slugs are abundant on most soils except coarse sand peats, whereas snails prefer soils overlying chalk or limestone where the calcium salts help to harden the shell.

Spider and Bryobia Mites
The red spider mite is a serious pest and large colonies of these minute creatures can build up causing severe damage to plants not only in the greenhouse, conservatory or house, but also outside. Bryobia mite attack is similar and plants show leaf mottling and bronzing which is often followed by complete leaf fall and death of the plant if the mites go undetected. Spider mites spin a fine webbing on plants, whereas bryobia mites do not.

Eelworms (nematodes)
Microscopic in size and of many different types some eelworms are parasitic, living in environments that include plants and animals. Others are 'free-living', some in the soil, others in water. They inhibit plant growth, can persist in the soil for many years and spread plant viruses. Gardeners should rotate their crops, always buy certified seed potatoes and certainly be cautious when offered plants, tubers and rhizomes for the garden.

Two winged, or true flies

Leatherjackets are the unattractive larvae of crane flies, or 'daddy long legs'. There are a number of species in the UK, all similar in appearance, differing only in the size of the adult insect. The commonest and the most usually seen is the grey crane fly, Tipula paludosa. Occasionally seen, both outside and in our homes, is the distinctly larger Tipula maxima. This crane fly has a more noticeable brown colouring with the light brown wing veining rather more pronounced. All the different crane fly species are equipped with two club shaped 'balancers', or halteres, positioned on the creature's body behind the two wings. They are believed to have developed from modified rear wings, and are there to stabilise the insect's flight. Females have a pointed rear to their abdomen, enclosing the ovipositor to lay their eggs whilst the male insect has a blunt and much more 'cut off' rear end.

The 'daddy long legs' is a familiar creature in the countryside, towns and our homes during spring, summer and autumn. Switch on the room lamps with the windows open on a warm summer night and in they come, dancing up and down the walls, unable to resist the lure of the light. In the house this is nothing more than an irritating nuisance, particularly as the crane flies can be somewhat difficult to catch. Despite losing one or more of their legs in our frantic efforts to catch them, they will persist in buzzing around up and down the walls and will do anything rather than go back outside. Those long legs, that seem to detach themselves so readily, have an especially important purpose for the crane fly, that of assisting the creature to lay its eggs in long grass.

Crane Fly larva - Leatherjacket

11

The crane fly is a fly of grassland, meadows and marshes, where breeding takes place. The eggs are laid, or just dropped, in the long grass and on the soil, and hatch into the larvae we know as leatherjackets. Small when hatched, the leatherjacket grows rapidly up to 4 cm in length. They are a dull grey brown colour with a tough and rubbery skin. Voracious feeders, they eat the roots of grasses and other plants at a phenomenal rate. At night, particularly in damp conditions, they will come to the surface and eat through plant stems at soil level. Vegetables as well as ornamental plants are often attacked, young plants and seedlings being killed outright, with damaged older plants prone to wilting in dry weather.

The leatherjacket is usually found in newly turned soil following grassland, and it is a particular pest of new gardens constructed on 'green field' sites. Infestations also occur in gardens where beds and borders are adjoining grass, and the pest may also be found in mature lawns. Lawns left to grow long during a wet period in the previous summer can be seriously damaged by crane flies taking the opportunity to lay their eggs into the longer than usual grass. Yellow patches appearing in lawns during a subsequent dry period should be investigated and the damaged area treated if leatherjacket feeding is suspected.

Leatherjacket Control

Control is either by thorough cultivation that exposes the leatherjacket to its natural bird predators or, if you don't mind picking them up, destroying them by hand! No soil insecticides are yet available for domestic use since the new EU directives on pesticides came into force. All gardeners hope that perhaps some newer and safer products will soon be available. Once any initial infestation in a new garden is cleared up, the leatherjacket is rarely an ongoing problem although it is wise to look for them in beds or borders adjoining lawns or grassland. Be prepared to expose the pest by cultivation if any numbers are found, the ground should be thoroughly dug over and left for a while for the birds to do their work.

Summary

- Check for leatherjackets where cultivations follow grass.
- Look out for yellowing dead patches in lawns, and temporarily lift the damaged turf to expose any leatherjackets
- If leatherjackets are found, thoroughly cultivate the soil and destroy the pest.
- During the mowing season try to keep grass cut short .
- Re-infestation is unlikely, except near grassland.
- If left uncontrolled damage is likely to be moderate to severe.

Sawflies

The larvae of these insects are often mistaken for caterpillars. Unlike caterpillars however the **sawfly** larvae have at least six pairs of false legs, placed towards the rear of their abdomen, behind the three pairs of jointed legs common to all insects. Caterpillars never have more than five pairs of these false legs. The name sawfly comes from the remarkable manner in which these insects lay their eggs. The egg laying tube, or ovipositor, is equipped with teeth similar to a minute saw. With this ovipositor

Gooseberry Sawfly

the sawfly is able to cut a slit in the leaf of a chosen plant into which it then inserts its eggs. Many hundreds of different species occur and some are notoriously damaging to our plants.

Apple trees are attacked by the **apple sawfly** and other fruit trees are hosts to two other common species. Fruit is often rendered unfit for eating with cavities eaten into the young flesh which develops into a decaying brown frass. Premature 'fruit-fall' of young developing apples is often caused by sawfly larvae damage.

Pear trees are commonly attacked by the **pear tree slugworm**, the voracious larva of the pear tree sawfly, damaging leaves by eating the top leaf surface and sometimes completely skeletalising them with a resultant reduction in fruit yield.

The common **gooseberry sawfly** is a very serious pest. The gooseberry bush is sometimes almost completely defoliated by the sawfly larva with consequent very severe loss of yield. The larvae are green with black spots and 35 mm in length. If this pest is discovered attacking the bush, prompt action is essential to prevent fruit loss.

Roses are sometimes attacked by the **leaf rolling sawfly**. In the Spring the eggs hatch and the larva feeds on the leaves which are drawn into tight rolls whilst the pest feeds. Treatment is by removing the rolled leaves and crushing them. It is rare for any chemical treatment to be needed for this particular sawfly. Polygonatums, such as Solomon's seal, are at serious risk from the dull grey larvae of the **solomon's seal sawfly**. They occur in groups of up to thirty or more on a leaf and can quickly defoliate an entire plant. **Derris**, or a **Bifenthrin** based insecticide, should be sprayed as soon as the grubs are seen.

Another of the sawfly order is the **wood wasp**, also referred to as a **horntail**, and sometimes as a **sirex**. Many people refer to them as hornets, because they are quite large, coloured black and yellow, and the females have a very long

Solomon's Seal Sawfly larvae

ovipositor. This is wrongly thought to be the creature's sting. This ovipositor is a powerful organ that can bore into soft wood where the horntail deposits its eggs. Horntails usually choose a conifer in which to lay their eggs. The hatched larvae then tunnel into the soft wood to feed. Control of this remarkable insect is not necessary and the horntail is totally harmless to man.

Sawfly Control

With all sawfly larvae it is well worth inspecting fruit trees and bushes for evidence of the caterpillar-like grubs during late spring, from mid April through to the end of May. If any of the grubs are found they should be dusted or sprayed with **Derris**, repeating this treatment at regular intervals as long as attacks persist.

Summary

- Inspect all fruit trees and bushes in early May. Check gooseberry bushes from April onwards.
- Always make 10 day checks on solomon's seal, and other polygonatums.
- If larvae are found, spray with either Derris (liquid), or a Bifenthrin based product.
- Re-check for any further larvae after 14 days, re-spray if necessary.
- If left uncontrolled, damage is likely to be severe or very severe.
- Do not mistake the horntail for a hornet, it will not sting you, and should not be killed.

Flies

The true flies Diptera are distinguished from other flying insects by having only one pair of wings. Unlike caterpillars their larvae have no legs and are often referred to as maggots. Cabbage root fly and carrot fly are both in this group of insects as are midges, gnats, mosquitoes and house flies, as well as crane flies.

Cabbage Root Fly

The **cabbage root fly**, similar in appearance to a housefly, is a common problem in vegetable gardens. All vegetables in the brassica family can be attacked by its larvae, particularly cabbages, brussels sprouts, cauliflowers, broccoli, turnips and swedes.

Cabbage Root Fly larvae

Especially at risk are seedlings after they have been transplanted into their permanent positions. When attacked the young plant wilts, developing a blue-red tinge, and in dry weather may die within a few days. When the plant is pulled up it can be seen that small white maggots, 6 - 8 mm long, are feeding on the root. More mature plants may also be attacked but, unlike young transplants, can stay alive though unlikely to ever properly recover.

Club root disease can also present similar leaf symptoms in brassicas so it is important to establish the cause as soon as possible by inspecting the roots of sickly plants for evidence of the small maggots. A natural method of control is to fit a plastic or cardboard disc around the stem at planting time, thereby preventing the female fly from laying her eggs in the soil surrounding the young plant. Redundant CDs are good for this purpose.

Carrot Fly

Unless a 24 hour watch is kept on the garden the adult is rarely seen. A small shiny black fly it is the larvae of this pest which causes trouble in the vegetable garden, particularly if carrots are grown regularly.

The first signs of an attack shows as a sudden bronzing of the leaves and poor growth of the plants. Other causes, such as motley virus and aphid attack, can produce similar symptoms in young carrot plants so further investigation is needed to determine the cause.

If the above symptoms are present the carrot root should be inspected. If the cause is carrot fly small white larvae, about 8 - 10 mm long and resembling small wireworms, will be found eating into the juicy flesh and tunnelling under the surface of the root.

15

Carrot Fly larva in carrot

If damage is occurring only to an odd individual plant, control measures are not really worthwhile and in any case, where infestation is not severe, the damaged parts of the carrot can be discarded when they are being prepared for cooking.

Carrot Fly Control

Prevention rather than chemical control is the best method of dealing with carrot fly. First a thorough cultivation of the proposed carrot patch during the winter will destroy any eggs and pupae. Then careful timing of the sowing date, after the end of May, will avoid the first generation egg laying of the adult female flies and for most gardeners this will be sufficient to minimise any attacks. It is nonetheless as well to remember that the fly is attracted to the scent of carrots so care must be taken to avoid bruising the plants when thinning them or when batch harvesting. To leave the remaining roots in the soil until later in the season is an invitation for a second generation of the fly to attack. Far better to lift the roots when reasonably mature and store them in peat for autumn and winter use.

Onion Fly

Onions, shallots and leeks growing in the garden are sometimes attacked by this fly. White maggots, up to 8 mm long, may be found in the leaves, stems, and sometimes within the onion bulb, causing the plant to eventually rot and die. Mid-summer is the time when damage is most noticeable. The damage should not be confused with onion white rot disease which produces similar symptoms of attack. White rot displays a fluffy fungal growth around the base of the stem and the bulb which does not occur with onion fly damage.

Onion Fly Control

Thorough cultivation of areas which have grown onions or leeks within the past two to three years will usually rid the soil of any over-wintering pupae of the fly and good crop rotation practices will keep attacks to a minimum.

Celery Fly

The **celery fly** is a leaf-mining pest and produces distinctive yellow blotches on the celery leaves, thereby weakening the plant and affecting both the appearance and ultimate maturity of the celery. Attacks become noticeable from late spring and can continue through until the autumn. The larvae of the celery fly, which are white maggots 5 –7 mm in length, pupate within the celery leaf or sometimes within the surrounding soil. Adults of this second generation then fly into the crop in the latter part of summer and commence egg laying occasionally giving rise to a third generation in the autumn.

Celery Fly Control

Control in the garden can be achieved by crushing both the larvae and pupae within the leaves. While plants are still very young a spray of **Bifenthrin** will give some protection though regular inspections of the crop should always be made from May onwards with crushing of the leaf mines if any are found.

Pear Midge

This **midge** is a small insect of around 3- 4 mm in size and very rarely seen. Though not a particularly common pest it can cause serious damage to developing pear fruit in May and June and often it is the same tree each year which is attacked. Fruit yield can be seriously depleted if infestations are allowed to go unchecked. In April or early May the females fly into the pear trees and lay their eggs in the young blossom buds. When the eggs hatch the many larvae enter the small developing fruitlets to feed. These fruitlets fail to develop properly and become blackened and distorted, falling from the tree prematurely with the pale yellow midge larvae inside the small malformed fruit. While this damaged fruitlet is on the ground the larvae enter the soil, spin their cocoons and are then dormant until they pupate in the following spring. The adult midge emerges in late March or April and often flies into the same tree that nurtured it the previous year to lay eggs in the flower buds and repeat the whole life cycle again.

Pear Midge Control

Control of this pest is best achieved by picking any affected fruits before they fall and keeping the ground beneath the tree free from any that have already fallen. This will greatly reduce the number of larvae that can enter the soil beneath the tree and thereby minimise subsequent attacks during the following year. The use of **Bifenthrin** for the control of fruit tree red spider mite may also control the female adult pear midge, but timing is very critical, and the spraying must be completed before the midges have a chance to lay their eggs.

Summary

- Protect the stem base of all cabbages, cauliflowers, brussels sprouts and other brassicas at transplanting time with 14 cm discs to prevent cabbage root fly egg laying.
- To control onion fly always thoroughly cultivate the soil before sowing or planting any of the onion family including leeks, onions and shallots and adopt a 3 or 4 year rotation of the beds.
- Regularly look out for symptoms of leaf-mining in young celery plants crushing, with finger and thumb, the larvae of the fly within the leaf.
- Bifenthrin sprayed on the young plants will give some protection.
- To minimise attacks of carrot fly thoroughly cultivate the intended seed bed, sow the seed after the end of May, and avoid bruising the plants at all times through to maturity.
- Pick any pears affected with pear midge before they fall and remove any that have fallen onto the ground.

Sciarids or 'Compost Flies'

Since the introduction of soil-less composts many years ago and the preponderance of peat-based composts, the **sciarid** has become a familiar insect, especially so in the greenhouse. These very small and delicate black flies are often seen running at high speed across the surface of the peat compost vibrating their wings as they go. When disturbed they may take to the air but soon return to continue their activity on the compost.

Also known as **mushroom flies**, the sciarids feed primarily on fungal material within the compost and soil. High temperatures in the greenhouse favour rapid breeding of the flies, when compost in seed trays etc is damp and ready for seed germination. Eggs laid by the female fly, sometimes approaching 100 in number, hatch after a few days into small, thin, white or nearly colourless larvae. They feed for a few weeks in the compost before pupation and emergence as adult flies. The very fine root hairs of recently germinated seeds are also sometimes included in the larval diet to the detriment of the young seedlings.

Sciarid Fly - Adult

Sciarid Control

Fortunately serious damage is unlikely except with the highest infestations. The nuisance value to the gardener is greater than any real damage and despite this the interesting and eccentric behaviour of the flies is something we can put up with. If this is not acceptable to the keen plantsman, the flies and their larvae are easily killed with most insecticides or a Fungus fly nematode can be used.

Psyllids

The **psyllid** is a sap-feeding winged insect which is able to both jump and fly and is equipped with two pairs of wings. The young nymph of this insect, known as a sucker, is also a sap feeder. Both the young and adults do considerable damage to young woody plants on leaves, buds and shoots. There are a number of species each having a different and specific host plant. The three species most likely to be encountered in the garden are the **apple sucker**, the **pear sucker** and the **bay laurel sucker**.

Psyllid Control

Control is best achieved by using a systemic insecticide spray. Unfortunately at the time of writing the most useful chemicals such as Dimethoate and Formothion have been withdrawn and even the valuable nonsystemic Malathion insecticide is no longer available. New systemic insecticidal products are no doubt in the pipeline and a watch should be kept on the garden centre shelves for suitable new products. In the meantime spraying

Pear Sucker psyllid

with **Bifenthrin** may give some control but will only affect suckers and adults by direct contact.

Ants

Of all the insects the gardener may encounter there are few that are as fascinating as the **ant** which have the most structured and remarkably intelligent social order. Our friends the bees come a very close second in this respect. In the garden the **black ant**, **Lasius niger**, is the most common, but the orange/brown **red ant**, **Formica rufa**, is also found in large numbers particularly in areas where the soils have a high sand content. All ants have strong jaws and can give gardeners a painful bite. Some species also carry a sting which can be painful though a bite from the ant is the most common injury. Ants have a very high nuisance value when they fly in swarms but are also responsible for some damage to our plants. Sometimes small pieces of leaf tissue are taken to feed themselves and seeds are also often taken from plants and seed-boxes as nutrition for their larvae. Seeds such as pansies, with a high oil content, are particularly at risk. Ants also cause considerable trouble by burrowing into the soil of our lawns and under border plants raising mounds of soil and depriving the roots of plants from the necessary moisture, often causing serious wilting. Indirectly they also contribute to aphid proliferation by 'farming' the aphids. This they do by stroking the aphids and tending for them, to obtain the honeydew the aphids exude and using it as food for themselves and their young. Sometimes the aphids are captured and brought to the ants nest where they are imprisoned, nurtured and unharmed, to provide a source of honeydew within the nest.

Patio paving is used by these insects where they construct nests in the sand under the paving. It is these nests, usually near the house, that are responsible for the influx of thousands of ants into our homes. At mating time swarms of flying ants emerge from these nests.

Ant Control

Good ant control requires locating the nests where the females, workers and young live in their many thousands, and then destroying it by liberally dusting the area with a **Pyrethrin** insecticide suitable for controlling crawling pests. This should be done as soon as the nest has been located.

Black Ant

Summary

- Check for damage from late spring onwards.
- Always keep pot plants and their composts free from dead leaves and other litter.
- With sciarids use Bifenthrin only if the infestation is severe.
- Watch out for new systemic insecticides on the garden centre shelves to control the three important garden psyllids. These are apple sucker, pear sucker and bay laurel sucker.
- To destroy Ants locate the nest and thoroughly dust the nest and surrounding area with a Pyrethrin dust, such as Permethrin. Alternatively, some success in eradicating the pest can be achieved by pouring boiling water directly onto the nest.

Pest Group 2

Butterflies and Moths

Of all the many species of moths and butterflies occurring in the UK most rely on wild plants for their food. The adults feed on nectar from flowers. Their young, the **caterpillars**, feed on leaves, stems, buds and flowers, with one or two species eating the roots of plants. Most of our butterflies are sun lovers, flying into our gardens by day, whereas the majority of moths fly by night. All are relatively strong fliers, some flying many hundreds of miles when migrating from one continent to another. Within the two thousand or so species recorded in this country only about 2% are known pests of garden plants, with perhaps ten of these having gained notoriety from the depredations of their caterpillars.

Large White Butterfly caterpillar

Large Cabbage White Butterfly

The **large cabbage white butterfly** is common in most gardens especially in areas where brassica crops are grown. The caterpillar damage from this species can be truly awesome if left uncontrolled, with row after row of plants reduced to skeletalised leaves and stems.

Large White Butterfly eggs

21

Even less severe attacks leave the plants disfigured with shredded leaves and the caterpillar excreta rendering the plants uneatable. The nasturtium is also often attacked and sometimes totally destroyed by the caterpillars of this species.

These caterpillars are distinctive, pale green and moderately hairy with black and yellow green stripes and grow up to 50 mm in length.

Severe infestations can occur at any time from May through to early October but are most likely in June, July and August. The large white butterfly often arrives in our gardens in groups of perhaps ten or more females with a few males in attendance. Clutches of up to 20 yellow eggs are laid on the brassica plants, usually on the underside of healthy leaves.

Small Cabbage White Butterfly

The **small cabbage white butterfly** caterpillars are easy to distinguish and are not quite so destructive as the Large White species. They are often very numerous in mid summer. Eggs are laid singly, sometimes on the upper surface of the leaves as well as below. These eggs hatch into plain, velvety smooth pale green caterpillars and can grow to a maximum of 30 mm in length. They are quite unlike the large cabbage white caterpillars.

Cabbage White Control

Whenever the white butterflies are seen it is sensible to check all plants of the cabbage family within the garden, inspecting the underside of all their leaves at least once per week. If the yellow eggs are found they should be rubbed out with the thumb. Take care not to damage the waxy cuticle of the cabbage leaf which is easily damaged if too much pressure is used.

If the caterpillars have already hatched and young ones are found clustered together, they can be crushed to eradicate them. If the caterpillars have grown larger and they can grow to 50 mm in length, then crushing is not really an acceptable option; it is much too messy and distasteful for most people.

Small White Butterfly Caterpillars

For any larger caterpillars on plants that are not yet badly damaged and still worth saving, a **Bifenthrin** spray can be used. Always spray both the top and the undersides of the leaves. A dusting of **Derris** is also an effective control.

vegetables. The **angle shades moth**, the **silver y moth**, and various **tortrix moths**, which spin silk webs to draw plant leaves together for protection, are all quite common and can cause a lot of damage if left uncontrolled.

Angle Shades, Silver Y and Tortrix Moths

Caterpillars of many moth species can also be troublesome in the garden. Though rarely causing as much damage as the cabbage white butterflies they can spoil the appearance of both flowers and

Angle Shades, Silver Y and Tortrix Moth Control

Inspecting plants regularly for caterpillars and their egg clusters is always worthwhile. Any found can then be removed and crushed. If many are found, a spray of **Derris** or **Bifenthrin** will eradicate them.

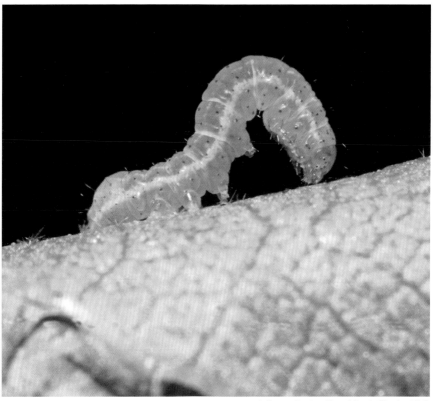

A "looper" caterpillar of Angle Shades Moth

Cutworms

The **turnip moth** and the **yellow underwing moth** have very damaging caterpillar larvae. These caterpillars live in the soil, devouring the roots of plants but they also come to the surface at night where they can then attack the stems of young plants, often severing them completely at soil level. Because of this type of damage they are often referred to as **cutworms**. Young vegetable seedlings are a favourite target and it is very disheartening when, expecting to see a neat row of young plants, one finds that 50-75% of them have their stems cleanly cut through at ground level with the remnants of the plants lying limp and wilting on the soil, the result of just one night's work by the cutworms.

Cutworm Control

Prevention is always better than cure and this applies particularly when dealing with cutworms. Good weed control and thorough autumn cultivations, especially on vegetable plots, will expose the caterpillars which can then be picked up and destroyed. Any that are missed will be found by birds and eaten with great enthusiasm.

In vegetable nursery beds it is good practice after initial cultivations

Common Cutworm

Ghost Swift Moth caterpillar in soil

to apply **Derris** insecticide to the soil, either as a spray or as dust. Alternatively dust the Derris along the seed rows after sowing.

Swift Moth

The **swift moth** is another species whose caterpillars live in the soil. Often seen when digging over soil at any time of the year, this is a distinctive white caterpillar with a shiny brown head, looking for all the world as though it has just been varnished. Smaller both in length and width than cutworms and chafer grubs they can reach a length of over 40 mm. These caterpillars feed below soil level on bulbs, tubers, plant roots, and rhizomes of many flowering plants and vegetables.

Swift Moth Control

Thorough cultivation, especially winter digging, will expose the larvae and pupae to light, which is harmful to them when young, and will also make them vulnerable to hungry birds.

Pea Moth

For gardeners who grow their own peas the **pea moth** is a species that occasionally causes trouble. When shelling your own garden peas it is quite disconcerting to find a small caterpillar within the shell eating the young peas. These marauders

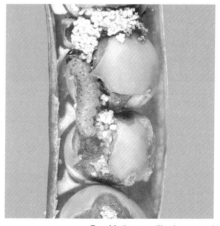

Pea Moth caterpillar in pea pod

25

are a very pale yellow in colour, almost white, with a black head.

Eggs of the pea moth are laid in mid June through to mid July, when adults fly to pea crops in warm sunny weather. The eggs hatch within 7 - 10 days and the emerging caterpillars eat into developing pods and feed on the young peas.

Pea Moth Control

Because of this relatively short period when the adult moths lay their eggs severe attacks can be minimised by sowing either early or late and avoiding sowing in March or April. If this is not possible **Bifenthrin** insecticide can be used when the peas flower in the June/July period. Make carefully timed sprays to coincide with the caterpillar hatchings, usually 7 - 10 days after flowering has begun. A follow-up spray 14 days later is advisable to destroy any caterpillars from later hatchings.

Other Moths

A number of other caterpillars are occasionally seen on trees and shrubs. Some, like the **codling moth**, are a particular threat to apple trees and are responsible for 'the maggot in the apple'. The **vapourer moth** has very hairy caterpillars, with highly distinctive markings of red and yellow lines. Buddleias and roses are often attacked but damage is not usually serious. The hairs of this caterpillar are very irritating to human skin, as is the case with many other hairy caterpillars to a greater or lesser extent, so care should be

exercised when handling them. The **magpie moth** larva is a 'looper' caterpillar, white with black and yellow markings, and can cause very serious damage to the leaves of gooseberries, very similar to gooseberry sawfly damage, with which it can be confused.

There are many other caterpillars which can occasionally be seen in our gardens. Some are very large such as the daunting **elephant hawk moth** larvae and some quite frightening with their grotesque appearance, such as the **puss moth** and **goat moth** caterpillars. Some are very small, often unnoticed until some damage is seen. Those listed are the most damaging and by far the most common on cultivated plants.

Control of Other Moths

Spraying with **Bifenthrin** will control moths with natural predators such as birds assisting us in our efforts.

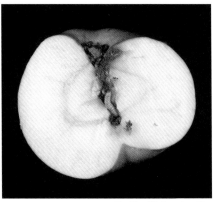

Codling Moth caterpillar

Magpie Moth caterpillar

Summary

- Remember to check all brassicas for butterfly eggs and caterpillars in early June and thereafter.
- Remove the caterpillars by hand if there are only one or two, and rub out the eggs.
- Severe attacks require a Derris or Pyrethrin based spray, or alternatively, a dusting of Derris powder.
- To control pea moth, spray the pea crop when the plants are nearing the end of flowering. Do not wait until flowering is finished.
- Check gooseberry bushes from April onwards for magpie moth caterpillars. They can be controlled with Bifenthrin.
- If left uncontrolled, damage can vary from moderate to very severe.
- Biological control can be achieved using a Caterpillar nematode.

Pest Group 3

Beetles, including the Earwig

Beetles (Coleoptera) are the largest family of insects and contain many species that are notorious pests in the garden. There are some that are beneficial to the gardener, as they are the predators of other smaller pests, thereby helping to maintain the orderly balance of nature. The well-known ladybird for example, and its larvae, consume vast numbers of aphids and should always be welcomed in the garden.

Of the various beetles, it is the larvae that are usually the most destructive to plants, though in a number of species the adult beetle can also do real damage.

Weevils of many different species are also members of the beetle family and around 500 species have been recorded in the UK. They are easily distinguishable from the ordinary beetle by the snout projecting from their head. Many are pests, particularly in their larval form. Most infamous of these at present is the **vine weevil**. This pest has proliferated over the past four or five years and gained well deserved notoriety due to the serious damage it can cause to our highly cherished house plants.

Common beetle & weevil pests
- Lily beetle
- Colorado beetle (not common but very dangerous)
- Asparagus beetle
- Chafer beetles
- Click beetle
- Flea beetle
- Raspberry beetle
- Strawberry seed beetle
- Vine weevil
- Pea & bean weevil

There are many, many others that may become pests locally, if not by causing direct physical damage, then certainly by the potential threat they carry of spreading virus diseases.

For identification purposes each of the above is described in the text separately, with photographs of some species of both the adult and its larva. Control measures can vary from seed dressings to spray chemicals and dust.

Lily Beetle

In warm weather, during early summer, the **lily beetle** becomes conspicuous in the

Lily Beetle

garden, attacking lilies and some polygonums.

At first sight, before damage to our plants becomes visible, the lily beetle is quite an attractive little insect, 5 - 6 mm long, coloured bright brick-red above and blackish underneath. If you try to pick him up he has a habit of deliberately falling off the leaf and hiding amongst the soil and litter beneath the plant! Both male and female adults feed on the leaves and stems.

Females lay up to 300 eggs, depositing them on the leaves of the lily. These eggs give rise to orange coloured larva, which quickly cover themselves with a black slime as soon as they start to feed. The larvae have an enormous appetite, shredding the leaves and leaving behind a quantity of disfiguring black slime and excrement.

Lily Beetle Control

Contact foliar insecticides, such as **Bifenthrin**, can be used to control the larvae and adults although it may be necessary to repeat this spraying if fine sunny weather leads to a re-infestation. The systemic insecticide, **Provado**, will also control both larva and adult. Any adult beetles you can manage to catch can be destroyed by crushing them between finger and thumb, although they are quite hard little insects and pressure from the thumb nail may have to be used.

Colorado Beetle

Although not often found in British gardens, I mention this pest briefly because the **colorado beetle** is sometimes inadvertently introduced on foreign produce imported into this country. Originating in North America, the beetle is alive and well in parts of mainland Europe, from where it is gradually spreading.

Larvae of Lily Beetle

Very distinctive in its smart colouring of black and yellow stripes. Measuring 10-12 mm long it is a very serious pest of the potato crop and other solanums, including tomatoes. The bright red larvae which feed on the plant leaves are also quite distinctive.

Colorado Beetle Control

In the UK any infestation or suspected sighting must, by law, be reported straight away to the Department for Environment, Food & Rural Affairs (DEFRA). The beetle and its larvae are voracious

Colorado Beetle on potato leaf

feeders of foliage and can quickly destroy whole potato crops if left unchecked. It is for this reason that the control and eradication of any outbreak of the pest is now the responsibility of DEFRA who can be contacted at:

Tel. 020 7238 6000
www.defra.gov.uk

Asparagus Beetle

Just as conspicuous as the colorado beetle with which it is sometimes confused because of its black and yellow colouring, is the **asparagus beetle**. It is much smaller however, rarely more than 6 mm in length, and is a much less serious pest in the garden than when the crop is grown commercially. The leaves and stems of the asparagus plant are eaten and the quality of the spears impaired. Severe attacks can seriously debilitate the plants.

Asparagus Beetle Control

Control is pretty straightforward. If the beetle or its larva becomes noticeable in spring, a dusting of **Derris** dust will get rid of both the pest and its larvae. This should be repeated if further attacks occur.

Chafer Beetles - Cockchafer

The largest of this family is the **cockchafer**, or **maybug**. Often it is seen, causing much surprise and consternation as it whirrs noisily past on warm evenings in May and June, sometimes even entering our houses after coming in through an open window. It is a large beetle, 25-30 mm long, and is often mistaken for a cockroach. Maybugs are in fact quite different in appearance and can be readily identified by their distinctive clubbed antennae and coppery brown wing cases.

The larvae of cockchafers are often found in the soil of old or neglected gardens and wherever turf has been lifted. Cochchafer larvae are large 40 mm in length C-shaped grubs with brown heads and soft, fat, creamy white bodies. They feed on roots, stems, bulbs, and tubers of vegetables and ornamental plants. Feeding within the soil under our lawns also causes damage and dead patches, very similar to the damage caused by leatherjackets. Depending on the availability of food the time taken to reach maturity and pupation can be up to four years though with the other smaller chafers pupation through to adult is usually complete within twelve months.

Cockchafer

Chafer Beetle Control

All the chafer grubs may be found whilst digging, especially on newly cultivated land and sometimes at

Cockchafer larva

considerable depths. They vary in size depending on species and stage of maturity, but the general appearance of the grubs is the same. Some of the grubs feeding nearer the surface are readily eaten by birds, and any that are exposed on the soil surface after cultivation will be quickly discovered and eaten.

Click beetles, wireworms

Wireworms are the larvae of **click beetles**, natural inhabitants of permanent grass pasture. The three common species in Britain, Agriotes lineatus, A.sputator and A.obscurus, seem to have decided preferences in where they will live and flourish. In the north of England obscurus is the dominant species, whereas in the south lineatus is the most abundant, with sputator being more common in the midlands. The appearance and way of life of all three species is very similar, as is the damage they cause to farm crops and to the plants in our gardens.

Click Beetle

The **click beetle** is quite an ingenious little creature. If one is laid on its back, or it happens to fall that way, it will struggle for a short while and then, with a quite audible 'click', jump into the air, and land again the right way up. It is a remarkable circus act, and always worth watching. It seems rather a shame that this engaging behaviour only lasts for around twelve months, the beetle's average life span as an adult. Before that, for the previous 4 to 5 years it has been in its larval state, a damaging wireworm.

In the garden, in conditions similar to those favoured by leatherjackets, wireworms are likely to occur where grassland has recently been cultivated. The beetle lays its eggs in the soil during spring and early summer. After they hatch the 1 mm sized young wireworms disperse into the soil, feeding on root hairs and other vegetation and growing steadily for 4 or 5 years. At this point they can be up to 30 mm long and ready to pupate in the soil, emerging some two months later in the autumn as the adult click beetle. Hibernation then occurs through the colder winter months and when the warm spring weather arrives the beetles emerge to start their remaining few months of life. Dispersing, mating and laying their eggs during the summer months they then die in the autumn and early winter.

Wireworms attack seedlings, bulbs and tubers of all types, especially potatoes, boring neat round holes into the tuber. These provide an

Click Beetle larva - Wireworm

entry hole for slugs, millipedes and other soil pests to consume the internal flesh. For farmers this pest can be a nightmare as whole crops of potatoes can be rendered unsaleable after an extensive wireworm attack.

Click beetle & wireworm control

Wireworms are easy to recognise when digging in the garden. They occur at varying depths but tend to live in the fertile top-soil where grass roots and the roots of other plants are present. Long, thin, and wiry, their colour varies from creamy white in the smaller young ones through to golden yellow to light brown in those that are more mature. They are easy to see in the soil and although agile and wriggly, they are not particularly quick to make their getaway. It is therefore an easy matter to pick them up and destroy them by crushing between finger and thumb assuming, of course, you are not too squeamish. Newly cultivated land can soon be cleared of any infestation by this method and re-infestation is very unlikely if the soil is under regular cultivation.

Flea Beetle - Adult

Flea Beetle

As their name implies, **flea beetles** are small insects of 2 - 3 mm long. There are a number of different species that attack garden plants of all types. Their larvae also feed on

Flea Beetle - Damage to radish

leaves and some attack the roots of seedling plants. In dry conditions and when the soil is warm the beetles can be easily seen scurrying down the rows of young plants and then settling on stems and leaves to feed.

Brassica plants, particularly young seedlings of brussel sprouts, turnips, cabbages and cauliflower, are all attractive food plants of the flea beetle. Small, neat round holes are made in the young leaves, checking the plants' early growth and disfiguring the crop.

April and May, especially when warm and dry, are when flea beetles are most active and when damage to young seedlings becomes noticeable. Vegetables and some flowering plants, especially any species closely related to brassicas, wallflowers and nasturtiums in particular, are susceptible to flea beetle attack.

Flea Beetle Control

Derris dust applied in warm dry weather to the leaves and the surrounding soil will effectively control both the flea beetle and the larvae should an attack occur.

Raspberry Beetle

Few things are quite so off-putting as finding a grub in a luscious raspberry when we are just about to eat it. Generally not apparent until the fruit is picked and being prepared for the table, the little grub is usually well inside the raspberry by the time the damaged surface of the fruit is noticed. The adult **raspberry beetle** is about 4 mm in size and flies onto the opening flowers of raspberries, blackberries and other cane fruit. The adult beetle does the damage to the flower, sometimes rendering it sterile and the female lays her eggs within the flowers. The eggs hatch within about two weeks and the newly emerged larval grubs feed on the developing fruit.

Raspberry Beetle Control

Control of the raspberry beetle is a matter of careful and correct timing. As soon as the main flowering period has finished the spray or dust control must be applied at the egg hatching stage or very soon afterwards. **Derris dust**, or a liquid **Derris spray**, is effective if properly applied. Also effective is a **pyrethrin spray** bearing in mind that the fruit must not be picked until the correct harvest interval after spraying has been allowed for if a more persistent product is used.

Strawberry Seed Beetle

Not usually a serious pest in the average garden the **strawberry seed**

Raspberry Beetle larva

beetle can cause extensive damage when the fruit is grown in any sort of quantity. The commercial strawberry grower is at a much more serious risk of fruit loss from this pest, as a considerable amount of the crop can be made unsaleable by the spoiled appearance of the fruit. Damage from the pest is very similar in appearance to bird damage and is equally difficult to control. Not many people are willing to buy or eat a strawberry that has a small chunk missing from it, whether it be from slugs, blackbirds or the strawberry seed beetle.

Strawberry Seed Beetle - Adult

If the strawberry seed beetle is suspected as being the cause of damage to the fruit then a very careful search of the straw or mulch beneath the plants may well reveal it as the culprit. This black ground beetle, which is usually about 15 to 20 mm in length, will often be discovered hiding amongst the plant debris and straw.

Strawberry Seed Beetle Control

Gardeners can help to prevent any possible attack on their fruit by **trapping** and destroying as many of the ground beetles as possible with the use of jam jars. These, half full of water, are sunk into the ground up to their rim at a number of stations within the strawberry bed. Once inside the jar, after falling into the water, these beetles can be collected and destroyed.

Vine Weevil

Within the last ten years or so the weevil family has become feared and hated to the point of paranoia in the mind of many gardeners. This reaction has been caused by the depredations of just one of its members, the vine weevil. Weevils of one sort or another, most of them recognised by the long snout-like projection from the head, have always been with us, damaging our plants, vegetables and flowers. The very rapid expansion of the house plant and container trade in both this country and Continental Europe has led to a corresponding and dramatic increase in the vine

Vine Weevil

35

Vine Weevil larvae

weevil numbers attacking our indoor plants.

The sudden collapse of a house plant is often the first sign of a vine weevil infestation. Providing the plant has enough moisture in the compost, is not saturated with too much water and has no sign on the leaves of disease or foliar pests, it is highly probable that something nasty is occurring to the roots of the plant. Evidence of vine weevil larvae should then be looked for within the compost.

The vine weevil larvae are rather like legless white maggots in appearance, and are usually between 6 – 8 mm long. They live in the compost, unseen and undetected, feeding on the plant roots. By taking the plant out of its pot a search can be made for them within the compost. Any that are found should be destroyed and provided there is still a reasonable degree of life in the plant, it should be re-potted

in clean container compost which has been treated with a drench of **Provado** insecticide. This will deal with any maggots which have been inadvertently missed during the root and compost inspection. **Provado** is a new systemic insecticide on the market, based on the chemical Imidacloprid, which is particularly effective in eradicating the weevil larvae in containers and pot grown plants. The product can be used as a compost drench as well as a foliar spray and is also now cleared for use on certain food crops grown under glass as well as on ornamental house plants growing in pots or other containers.

Adult weevils of this species are creatures of the night, hiding in soil litter, walls and woodwork during daylight hours. Vine weevils are unusual in being nearly all females. They are parthenogenetic and able to reproduce by laying a prodigious number of viable eggs without the intervention of the very rare males

Vine Weevil Control
Cleanliness in the garden and greenhouse will do a great deal to ensure that the weevil adults do not become a problem. If the adult weevils do occur in any numbers **Provado** can be used to control them, or alternatively, the natural product **Derris** which can be used either as a dust or a spray.

Pea and Bean Weevil
Pea and pean weevils are common and quite prolific insects attacking many other plant species as well as peas and beans and other

leguminous plants such as lupins. They are somewhat shy, retiring creatures and difficult to catch, dropping from the leaves to hide in the soil if disturbed. The weevil damage to broad beans in particular is very distinctive and easy to recognise. When an attack has occurred, the bean leaf, normally having a smooth and unbroken margin to the leaf, will be found to have 'scalloped' edges all the way round the leaf margin, looking for all the world as though it was normal and meant to be like that. Sometimes quite tall mature plants are so severely infested that the majority of the leaves have signs of having been bitten. This is not too serious on the older bean plant, but can be debilitating with potential future yield loss when it occurs on younger, smaller plants. This damage from the adult weevil is only a part of the story. Eggs laid in the soil hatch into larvae which feed on the roots of the leguminous plants before pupating and later emerging as adults.

Pea & Bean Weevil damage to broad bean leaves

Pea and Bean Weevil Control

Prevention is better than cure so careful garden hygiene to remove litter on the soil and in particular, ensuring a clean, fine seed bed, will do much to deter the female weevil from egg laying and also deny the weevil a place to hide. If an attack has occurred it is worthwhile dusting or spraying the plants with **Derris** to minimise further damage. If the black bean aphid is also present on the plants a good spray insecticide such as **Bifenthrin** can be used as an alternative.

Summary

- Where damage from beetles and their larvae are occurring, or expected, dust with Derris (rotenone) around the plants or along the rows.
- A Bifenthrin spray is equally effective, on both adults and their larvae.
- If left uncontrolled damage can vary from slight to severe.
- Unthrifty potted plants, with no signs of pests or disease, should have their compost and roots checked for vine weevil larvae. If any are found drench the compost with a solution of Provado. Vine weevil may also be controlled biologically with a weevil nematode.
- Report any sightings of colorado beetle to DEFRA.

Earwigs

Earwigs

To many people, the sight of an **earwig** gives them the creeps. Most of us would recognise one, if only because of those telltale pincers at the rear end of its body. No, it does not climb into your ear and bite away the eardrum, but it may well find its way into your ear if you have been lying on grass or rough ground, not to bite or feed upon you, but to hide snugly from its enemies in warmth and darkness.

There are two common British species, although some foreign species have become established in southern England, sometimes arriving on imported vegetables and fruit. These colonies do not persist for very long, except perhaps in glasshouses, as they are less winter hardy than our native species.

It is not always realised that the earwig is a true insect with wings and fully able to fly although they rarely fly except at night. It is the smaller of our two common species

that is more ready to take to the air than its slightly larger cousin. Both species prefer to run away from trouble, which they can do with some alacrity, rather than take to the air. Earwig wings are very fine membranes and quite large for such a relatively small insect, requiring many, many folds to get them tucked away out of sight under the front wing cases, or elytra.

Eggs are laid in soil in the winter and hatch in early spring. The mother earwig is a most conscientious insect. She dutifully stays with her brood of young, the nymphs, feeding and caring for them with the utmost diligence until they can fend for themselves above ground in late spring.

Generally keeping out of sight during the day the earwig hides in dark secluded places such as cracks in wood, masonry, the bark of woody plants and the young unopened leaves of many herbaceous plants.

It is at night when the earwig climbs into our prize blooms of dahlias, chrysanthemums, zinnias and many other flowering plants, chewing the petals, eating into unopened buds and leaves and generally making a complete nuisance of itself. Often the culprit, gorged with feeding, will decide to stay and hide during the daylight hours in the ragged ruin of the bloom it has consumed during the previous night.

In fairness it should be admitted that the earwig will also feed to a limited extent on some small pests such as aphids, mites etc, but that is small consolation for the damage they undoubtedly cause.

Earwig Control

Good garden hygiene and tidiness is vital in any attempt to limit earwig damage. (I make no apologies for continually harping on about garden tidiness and hygiene. It is an important message that should be heeded by all keen gardeners.)

Decaying matter such as woody rubbish, old sacking, old wooden seed boxes and any areas of the garden that are left derelict should be thoroughly cleared and cleaned up. Regular cultivation, hoeing etc is necessary to destroy egg laying sites and the provision of some form of earwig traps, placed amongst susceptible plants, will limit the damage that may otherwise be done by these insects.

A useful and not too unsightly trap can be made by stuffing a 3" or 4" plant pot with hay or straw and placing it, upturned, on a bamboo cane, at the same height as the flowers it is intended to protect. By day, the earwig will climb into the trap to hide. Each evening, before dark, they can be collected from the trap and destroyed.

Where plants are infested a spray of an insecticide such as **Bifenthrin** can be used, spraying at dusk, when the earwigs are likely to be active and bee activity has ceased.

Known breeding sites around the house or outbuildings can also be dusted with an insecticidal powder. I should stress once again that, as with many garden pests, total control of earwigs is never likely to be achieved, and of course complete eradication is neither justified nor environmentally desirable. However trapping and good garden hygiene will keep any damage to an acceptable level.

Summary

- Use the 'straw in a pot' trap.
- Dust cracks and crevices with a pyrethrin dust, such as Permethrin
- Remove plant litter regularly.
- If left uncontrolled damage is likely to be moderate.

Pest Group 4

The True Bugs

Aphids

Aphids belong to the enormous group of true plant bugs. They are one of the most successful families of insects and have a quite remarkable life cycle, with an ability to reproduce themselves both by laying eggs, and by giving birth to live young. Not only that, they can reproduce themselves both sexually and asexually, without the intervention of the male. Aphids can be winged or wingless, though because of their small size and very light weight, they are not strong fliers. Aphid infestations can occur with surprising speed on garden

Rose Aphid on developing bud

plants and in fields when conditions for their migration and breeding are favourable. Clouds of aphids can be carried on winds and thermal currents, sometimes from hundreds of miles away, suddenly descending and colonising our gardens and surrounding farm crops.

There are very many different aphids with around 500 species occurring in the UK. They are commonly known as **greenfly** and **blackfly** but their colour varies greatly depending on species. Often suddenly discovered on young stems and flower buds many plants are at serious risk from them in dry, warm conditions. With their ability to puncture leaves and stems they feed by literally 'plugging in' to the sap stream pressure of the plants and with little further effort,

Black Bean Aphid

Red Ant and Aphids

ingest the nutritious sap that flows into them.

Some aphids are very selective feeders and only attack one particular species of plant. Others are not so choosy, happily feeding on many different types of plants, vegetables, and woody shrubs, including apples and other fruit and forest trees.

The physical damage caused by this feeding seriously debilitates the plant and can cause the death of immature plants and seedlings if the infestation is severe. The excreted sticky 'honeydew' the aphid leaves behind also disfigures the plant and results in fungal sooty moulds

developing on the leaves. This black mould greatly reduces assimilation of the light striking the leaves and can seriously slow down the ability of the plant to manufacture sugars by photosynthesis.

More importantly perhaps, the aphids often carry virus plant diseases in their mouth parts and saliva, having picked up these viruses from previously feeding on an infected plant. Virus transmission by the aphid can be the most serious potential risk of any infestation.

Aphid Control
The aphid has many natural predators which help to keep this

Plum Aphids

pest within manageable numbers. Ladybirds and their greyish blue larvae, various hoverflies, and the beautiful lacewings, together with some parasitic wasps, all contribute to reducing the aphid population. Small birds also consume large numbers at certain times of the year.

Environmentally it is sound practice to use insecticides only when absolutely necessary. However for serious infestations it is vital, for the health of the plant, to quickly and effectively eradicate this pest. For a minor attack of say half a dozen or so aphids per plant, washing them off the leaves and buds with soapy water may well suffice, though the use of an effective aphicide is imperative for the control and eradication of a more severe infestation.

Due to new EU regulations only **Bifenthrin** is approved for ornamental plants and some named vegetables and fruits. Product labels should always be carefully read as not all formulations are the same despite having the same active ingredient. As these products have a very short 'harvest interval' between the spraying and picking of food crops, their use is preferred when dealing with aphid infestations in the fruit and vegetable garden. A relatively new product, **Provado**, based on the active ingredient **Imidacloprid**, is also an effective aphicide as well as controlling a number of other pests and has the advantage of being a systemic product.

For ornamental plants that are flowering great care should be taken to spray either in the early morning, or just before dusk, to safeguard the bee population. It is also important, regardless of the product used, that the spray is directed away from any open flowers wherever possible, not only for the sake of the bees but also to prevent any damage to the pollination mechanism

Summary

- Check weekly for aphids outdoors, February to November. A weekly check of indoor or protected plants should be made throughout the year.
- Severe infestations - spray with Bifenthrin insecticide or Provado.
- Light infestations - wash off the aphids with soapy water.
- When spraying avoid open flowers and protect beneficial insects.
- Pinch out the tops of maturing broad bean plants, to minimise black bean aphid infestation.
- If left uncontrolled damage is likely to be moderate to severe.

Thrips

Thunder bugs or **thunder flies**, as the many species of **thrips** are commonly known, are a very common irritation to gardeners, getting into their ears, nose and hair when gardening on hot, humid days. They are also pests of many plants when they occur in large numbers, which they usually do, affecting the appearance of leaves and flower buds. The damage they cause is quite similar to, and can be mistaken for, spider mite damage with plant leaves having a silvery, mottled appearance. This silvering is particularly noticeable on peas and sweet peas, and also gladioli, where the waxy cuticle of the leaf

Adult Gladiolus Thrip

has been damaged by thrip feeding. Very severe attacks result in the disfiguring of the plant, though this is rare in this country other than in exceptionally hot summers.

There are many different species of thrip but four or five of these are the common types found in our gardens and greenhouses. The **glasshouse thrip**, the **onion thrip**, the **gladiolus thrip**, and the **rose thrip** are all capable of annoying our plants and us.

Thrip Control

Occasional and light infestations are not usually worth treating as damage is unlikely to be severe. Where serious and continuing infestations occur control is straightforward using a **Bifenthrin** insecticide as a spray. In the garden, when weather conditions favour thrip swarms, it is advisable to wear clothing of a dark or subdued colour. Wearing bright colours, particularly white or yellow, will guarantee you being the target of all the thrips in your vicinity, with the consequent discomfort that they will cause.

Froghoppers

Nearly all of us, especially those of us living in rural areas, will have heard the term **cuckoo spit**. Flowering grasses in the hedgerows and elsewhere during May are often seen to have blobs of frothy 'spit'

Thrip damage on gladiolus leaf

on their leaves and stems. This 'spit' is manufactured and exuded by a little sap sucking insect, the **froghopper**, to shield and protect it as it feeds on the plant's sap. Not unlike a large aphid, and a true bug of a bright, pale green colour, the young froghopper nymph is only discovered if the froth is wiped or washed away.

As well as grasses, many other garden plants play host to this insect with young plants being rather debilitated by the froghopper's feeding. Damage is rarely if ever serious; more it is a case of the garden looking unsightly if a number of plants are affected.

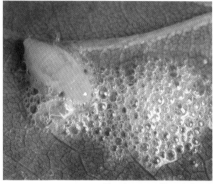

Froghopper - Nymph & spit

Froghopper Control

Spraying away the froth and the froghopper nymph with water from the hosepipe is all that is needed to restore the garden to its immaculate best again. Very easy.

Capsids

Sap sucking insects of many different species belonging to the **miridae** family feed on many garden plants and fruit trees, with the **green capsid** and the **apple capsid** being perhaps the most common. Damage to leaves, buds and flowers is caused by both the winged adults and the immature, wingless nymphs. Small and untidy holes on leaves and shoots, which are very similar to flea beetle damage, should be investigated immediately though finding the culprits is often difficult. Both the adults and nymphs are quick to sense danger and either fly away or fall to the ground if disturbed. Capsid damage to flowers can be mistaken for earwig damage as

Common Green Capsid

similar symptoms of missing or torn petals appear when developing buds have been attacked.

Adult capsids lay eggs during the autumn on woody plants such as apple and other fruit trees. The eggs hatch in spring with the young nymphs feeding on the new growth of the woody host before moving to herbaceous plants. Here the nymphs mature into winged adults with the females laying eggs during mid summer, giving rise to a second generation of the pest.

Capsid Control

Control of these insects is not easy although if capsid attacks can be confirmed spraying the affected plants with a good insecticide can go some way to defeating the pest. A second spray may be needed if attacks continue during the summer months. Ideally a systemic insecticide should be used if available giving a longer period of control. The precaution of clearing up decaying plant matter in the beds and borders, as a regular routine, will also help to keep infestations at a low level.

Summary

- Both nymphs and adults are susceptible to insecticide sprays.

- Always check for damage from late spring onwards.

- Nymphs and adults of both thrips and capsids can be controlled with Bifenthrin if there is a build up of these pests.

- A gentle jet of water is all that is required to wash away the frothy spit, with the froghopper nymph inside, and no insecticide is needed.

The following are a collection of bugs that are perhaps a little less common in the average UK garden and greenhouse. All of them are capable of causing damage to our plants if they occur in any quantity with some, such as the mealybugs causing more damage than the others.

Leafhoppers

As the name **leafhopper** suggests these insects are often noticed on leaves, jumping and flying from one

Leafhopper

leaf to another. A number of different species of leafhoppers live in gardens and in greenhouses and all are capable of disfiguring individual leaves of many plants. Roses, ornamental beech trees, apple trees, potatoes and cane fruit such as raspberries, are all favoured by these insects. In the greenhouse tomatoes and many different

ornamental plants can also be quite seriously damaged. Hot, dry conditions suit the leafhopper very well and most damage occurs in the midsummer months.

Leafhopper nymphs

Leafhopper damage usually shows as a whitish mottling of the upper surface of the leaves with the immature leafhopper nymphs and cast skins easily seen on the underside of the leaves.

Leafhopper Control

Where infestation is severe premature leaf fall can occur and it is important to control this pest before this stage is reached. Bifenthrin will give good control and should be applied immediately the pest damage is seen avoiding as always the spraying of any plants that are in flower.

Leafhopper damage on tomato

Mealybugs

These are sap-sucking insects of a number of different species. Many cultivated and wild plants suffer attacks from this pest, though the most noticeable infestations occur with the **glasshouse mealybug** in greenhouses and on pot plants within the home.

Mealybugs

About 3 - 4 mm in size, the female insect is without wings and has a rounded body covered in a white waxy powder with hair-like filaments. The mealybugs cluster together in colonies on different parts of the plant, such as leaves, stems and flowers and often form these colonies on inaccessible parts of the plant such as the leaf axils and around opening flower buds. As with aphids and whiteflies, which are also sap-suckers, they debilitate the plant as well as exuding sticky honeydew which fouls the leaves and stems giving rise to the growth of sooty moulds.

Mealybug Control

Very severe infestations require drastic measures. Chemical control is far from easy due to the protective layer of wax covering the insects. Biological control can be tried, using **Cryptolaemus larvae**, though it is often best to cut out the affected parts of the plant and consign these to the bonfire.

Scale Insects

About ten different species of **scale insects** are common pests of many plants, shrubs and trees. Females and their young, the nymphs, settle down to feed on the plant sap, usually on the underside of leaves. They cover themselves with a waxy scale for protection and are relatively static. The scale is usually a light brown colour with a darker centre, although scale colour varies with the particular species. The

Scale insects

47

oleander scale, for instance, which attacks many different plants, has a scale looking for all the world like a tiny, 2 mm fried egg.

Greenhouse plants including orchids, peach trees, camellias, begonias, figs and carnations are just some of the hosts which can support the scale insects. In fact, as with many pests, protected cultivation favours their establishment and survival.

Scale Insect Control

Scales can easily be removed from house plants and plants with tough leaves, by simply washing them off with a small brush dipped in really soapy water. For plants with smaller foliage and for shrubs and small trees which are infested, a spray of **Bifenthrin** insecticide is effective in controlling the nymphs, with a second spray two weeks later to destroy any that are newly hatched. The scale insect eggs are protected by the waxy scale, so it is essential to time the two spray applications at the optimum egg hatch times which occur in

late spring and early summer. Biological control is also available for greenhouse use only using the predator **Chilocorus nigritus**.

Whiteflies

Two common species occur in this country, the glasshouse whitefly, and the cabbage whitefly. Other species of this family are occasionally seen, one infesting rhododendrons and another species attacking evergreen azaleas. All are similar in appearance, white, moth-like insects, very small, about 2 mm long and easily recognisable. When disturbed they take flight, often in large numbers, before resettling on the top and undersides of leaves. When whiteflies are at rest their four wings are folded back over the body, giving the insect a small, moth like delta shape.

As well as very seriously debilitating the host plants by their feeding they exude honeydew in a similar manner to aphids which leads to the colonisation of affected plants by sooty moulds. Tomatoes, aubergines, peppers, house plants

Summary

- Always keep pot plants and their composts free from dead leaves and other litter.

- Use Bifenthrin for controlling scale insects.

- With leafhoppers use Bifenthrin only if the infestation is severe.

- For mealybug control, Cryptolaemus larva is an effective parasite, but severe attacks may require the destruction of the affected parts of the plant.

and other flowering ornamental plants in the greenhouse are often severely infested with whiteflies, spoiling the appearance of the plants and seriously weakening them. Unless quickly controlled this pest can proliferate extremely rapidly and becomes almost impossible to eradicate. I know of one glasshouse crop of tomatoes where control was delayed because only a small number of whiteflies were noticed. When it was decided that control was necessary everything the grower had available was used. **Bifenthrin** and some other insecticides, including the now banned old standby Malathion, were tried with little success, each and every one of these applied strictly according to the label instructions and repeated with follow up sprays. The predatory **Encarsia wasp**, was then tried for a period of six weeks, again with little noticeable improvement. After five months, whiteflies were still in evidence in that glasshouse and were only completely cleared at the end of the season, when all plants were removed and sulphur smokes were used as part of the annual clean up and sterilisation.

The life cycle of the whitefly commences with the adult laying

Whitefly - adults

49

up to 200 eggs on the host plant, usually on the underside of the leaf. These then hatch into the nymphs, which move over the plant for a short period before settling down to feed. After losing legs and antennae the pest then becomes a static scale and in that state continues to feed for 10 to 14 days. The scale then ceases to feed and starts the process of pupation, leading to the emergence of the adult whitefly. At high temperatures such as occur in greenhouses or in settled summer weather this whole cycle from egg to adult can be completed within three to four weeks, although in lower temperatures below 60°F, the process takes much longer.

Whitefly Control

As with aphids, whiteflies are parthenogenetic, although sexual reproduction does also take place. Because of this life cycle the control of whiteflies is not easy and made rather more difficult in recent years by the growing resistance of the pest to chemical sprays. Glasshouse whitefly in particular has become resistant to organo-phosphorus sprays previously used by gardeners. In most areas **Bifenthrin** is still effective at present although resistance to this product is now beginning to occur. Many commercial growers are turning to biological control in heated glasshouses using the parasitic predator Encarsia formosa to control the pest. Supplies of this predator are available for domestic use but the use of Encarsia for pest control is not by any means easy. The Encarsia parasitic wasp must be introduced before whitefly populations become too great though conversely there must be enough whitefly to ensure the Encarsia does not die from lack of food. When using any form of biological control such as this, chemical insecticides against other pests must be used with caution in order to safeguard the predator.

Summary

- Always watch out for this pest, particularly under glass, but also on cabbage plants, azaleas and rhododendrons.
- If seen, spray immediately with Bifenthrin insecticide, repeating twice, at 7 day intervals, to control newly hatched adults.
- In the greenhouse, spray as above, or use Encarsia formosa, a parasite of the whitefly.
- Always act quickly to prevent populations getting out of control. Subsequent damage can be very severe.
- Trap the whitefly with yellow sticky traps in the greenhouse, to monitor the population levels occurring.

Woodlice, Millipedes, Springtails and others

Woodlice

Although the **woodlouse** is a well known inhabitant of most gardens, to many of us they are particularly unattractive creatures and we are inclined to fight shy of dealing with them. Often referred to as 'insects' they are actually a terrestrial species of crustaceans which contains many familiar marine species such as shrimps, prawns, crabs and lobsters. Woodlice have up to seven pairs of legs, depending upon their age and stage of development, but despite this they generally move relatively slowly, although they can get a considerable move on if danger threatens. They usually congregate in large numbers wherever leaf litter, decaying wood and dead plant material is left lying around, both indoors and out, such material not only giving them shelter but also forming the bulk of their diet.

Sad to say they do not always confine themselves to such unappetising fare and do attack living plants in our gardens and greenhouses from time to time. They are rarely seen doing any damage, usually preferring to eat their meals after dark.

Enjoying moist, humid conditions, they are most happy in damp and warm greenhouses and plant houses with low brick walls upon which they can climb in search of food. These also provide plenty of hiding places in loose or missing mortar.

Both in the garden and greenhouse any plants growing on or near walls are particularly at risk, especially when plant litter has been left on the ground.

Damaged leaves with untidy edges and irregular holes bitten into them should always be investigated and any leaf litter nearby searched for the pest. Young seedlings in seed boxes are often damaged, the woodlice cleanly severing the stems of the young plants. Damage is similar to earwig attack although woodlice, unlike earwigs, rarely attack flowers and flower buds preferring instead to chew the margins of leaves.

Woodlice control

Control of woodlice starts with good hygiene, both under glass and in the open garden. Any areas where plant litter is left lying on the ground can become potential hiding places for them during the day. The underside of old seed boxes, stones and decaying wood provide them with shelter and allow colonies

Adult Woodlouse

to build up and threaten nearby plants.

Unfortunately the woodlouse has very few natural enemies. Insect eating birds and mammals tend to leave them well alone due to a foul secretion they exude when handled or attacked. The smell from a dead colony of woodlice can be truly appalling unless they are cleared out of the way before they decompose. Boiling water poured onto the colonies quickly kills them but for the squeamish who might find this method distasteful, they can be killed by poisoning with a persistent insecticidal dust such as **Permethrin** which is often also used as an ant killer.

Summary

- Good garden hygiene is most important.
- Remove litter, particularly decaying wood.
- Destroy colonies with boiling water or crush underfoot.
- If left uncontrolled damage is likely to be light to moderate.

Millipedes

Sometimes mistakenly referred to as centipedes the **millipede** is often found inhabiting the heavier soils where the organic matter is fairly high. Unlike centipedes the millipede, though wriggly, is a relatively slow moving soil pest. It has a segmented body with two pairs of legs on each segment whereas the centipede has only one pair of legs per segment. Four members of the family are common in gardens; the **black millipede**, the **spotted millipede**, and the two **flat millipedes**, these latter two bearing a superficial resemblance to centipedes due to their flatter shape and variable light colouring. They can also move more quickly than the black millipede. In common with centipedes and woodlice the millipede always favours moist soils, particularly those with a high humus content.

As a garden pest millipedes are rarely if ever a serious problem and many of them pass unnoticed in the soil until a tuberous crop such as the potato is grown. When harvesting what looks like an apparently clean and healthy crop of potatoes the millipedes' work may be discovered. Good well-formed and healthy tubers may be found to have neat 2-3 mm holes drilled into them. When the holed

Snake Millipede

potato is cut open, a great deal of hollowing of the internal flesh may well have taken place, sometimes with the culprit caught red handed still inside the tuber. Occasionally the offender can turn out to be a keeled slug but often it is the work of one or more black millipedes

The neat holes in bulbs, corms and tubers caused by wirewoms and other pests are often enlarged by both slugs and millipedes, which thereby gain access to a lifetime

food supply. Seeds and young seedlings of many flower and vegetable plants are also often attacked by the millipede both in the garden and the greenhouse.

However, cultivated plants are not the main food source of millipedes. Much of their diet consists of dead and decaying matter in the soil so control of the pest starts with thorough cultivation and the removal of dead plant debris from garden beds and borders.

Black Millipede

Millipede control

If a garden is found to have an infestation, then control can be achieved thorough cultivation, thereby exposing the millipedes for the birds to feast upon, or by picking them up by hand and destroying them.

Summary

- Good garden hygiene is required.
- Thorough and regular cultivation is most important.
- Do not confuse with the larger 'tan coloured' centipedes.
- If left uncontrolled damage is likely to be slight or moderate.

Springtails

Although very common and widespread, particularly on acid soils, detectable damage from the **springtail** is not always easy to confirm. Varying in size from 1 or 2 mm, with some species achieving 4 mm, they are often mistaken for fleas due to their jumping can damage plants by eating very small holes in young leaves at ground level and also by feeding on fine root hairs just below the soil surface. Pot plants in the house and under glass occasionally harbour one or two springtails and it is in this environment where they may be mistaken for fleas.

Immature Springtail

capabilities. Their main source of food is dead plant material and fungal mycelium, naturally abundant in most soils. Where they occur in large numbers they

Springtail Control

Control with insecticides is rarely necessary although **Bifenthrin** can be used. Cleanliness in the removal of decaying plant material both in the garden and the greenhouse is essential to prevent the build up of damaging numbers.

Symphylids

The symphylid is a soil dwelling arthropod and is related to centipedes and millipedes. It is a very small creature, rarely more than 5mm in length, though the size can vary between 3 and 10 mm depending on its age and the number of times it has moulted. Each moult, when completed, adds an extra segment or two to its body length.

Due to a life spent in the depth and darkness well below soil level it has a colourless and translucent appearance and is quite eyeless. It is nonetheless adept in finding its way around the soil particles in search of food, achieved by using the small antennae on its head and possibly also from the scent of decaying matter which is the symphylid's main food source. Fine root hairs are also consumed and it is in an agricultural context when this root feeding can become a problem unless known infested fields are first treated with an insecticide before drilling the crop.

In the garden however it is rare for this creature to cause a problem, except when greenhouse border soils become infested. Soils of a high pH value, such as those overlying chalk, appear to support the larger symphylid populations and young, transplanted tomato crops in particular can suffer stunted growth if the symphylid is present. No soil insecticides are available for domestic use, although the pest can usually be eradicated if the soil is regularly, and frequently, subjected to deep cultivation.

Slugs and Snails

Not 'bugs' of course, but slugs and snails are included in this list of harmful garden creatures because of the very serious damage they can inflict on our plants. Belonging to the mollusc order, they are very common throughout the British Isles and easily recognised. What is not generally appreciated is just how many different types of **slugs and snails** there are. Which are the most voracious feeders and which plants do they prefer?

Garden Snail

55

All slugs and snails move by muscular contraction of the underside of their body, the 'foot', at the same time producing slime, which assists them to move slowly but easily on many different soil and plant surfaces.

Slugs are not too particular where they live, some existing quite happily within the soil while others prefer the soil surface. They are abundant on most soil types except coarse sands and some peats. Snails are always much more in evidence on the calcareous soils, such as those overlying chalk or limestone, the calcium salts playing a part in the production and hardening of the snail shell.

Although hermaphrodite, possessing both male and female organs, reciprocal cross fertilisation does take place with both slugs and snails resulting in clutches of small translucent eggs, like miniature pearls, being laid in the soil. Eggs

Grey Field Slug

hatch in about a month producing small but very damaging young.

Ground beetles of many species, of which well over 300 occur in the UK, while being unable to eat adult slugs and snails, do much to help the gardener by eating these eggs and thereby reducing in some measure the overall population levels.

Slugs and snails feed above and below ground always avoiding bright warm sunshine which can dehydrate them. They are most active when humidity is high, and especially so at night when temperatures are lower. The slime trails glistening on plant foliage and on the soil are usually the first noticeable sign that our plants are being eaten. The vast amount of damage they can inflict in just one night is very disheartening to the keen gardener, with shredded leaves apparent, the stems of young seedling plants eaten through, and sometimes whole boxes of seedlings destroyed within a few hours.

The very large, fat, **black slug** (Arion ater) is a very common creature in most gardens and when mature can reach a length of 15 cm and be 2 cm wide. This slug produces copious amounts of slime and is easily seen but thankfully it rarely attacks cultivated plants. Related brown and orange species of equal size are often found around house walls, and sometimes even indoors in damp areas around doorways, airbricks in walls and similar sites.

Of far greater importance in the garden is the **black keeled slug**, growing up to 2 cm long. This slug tends to curl into a sickle shape when disturbed. Often feeding below ground, it is very damaging to potatoes, other tubers and many bulbous plants.

Equally destructive, and probably the most common slug in gardens and grassland, is the **grey field slug**. The name can be misleading as the great majority of this species are a light fawn colour and equally at home in our gardens as they are in fields. Varying in size from 3 - 5 cm they are a most unwelcome and voracious pest, eating both cultivated and wild plants, including grass species in lawns and paddocks. Slugs consume our leafy vegetables with enthusiasm. In particular, our cabbages, sprouts, and other brassicas are always at risk, providing truly sumptuous meals for them.

Slug and Snail Control
As with all garden pests careful attention to good garden hygiene is the starting point for their control. Both slugs and snails thrive in areas where the organic matter in the soil is high. They congregate and hide under plant litter within the soil, under stones etc, in fact anywhere that provides shade from the sun and protection from predators. These predators are many. Birds of many species large enough to handle them will greedily relish the succulent meal they provide, the shell of snails offering little protection from the ingenuity of

thrushes, blackbirds etc, in using a stone to crack open the shell to eat the snail dwelling inside. Hedgehogs and moles also consume a large number in both fields and gardens. Yet despite the many and varied numbers of creatures which feed on them, slugs and snails continue to proliferate and to this day it has to be admitted that only partial control can ever be achieved.

Rough soil conditions give them some shelter so a fine tilth in the border soil will deter the pests to some extent. In the garden various forms of trapping can be used, the slugs or snails then removed by hand and destroyed. Traps range from straight sided containers filled with beer and sunk to rim level into the soil to various fruit traps such as half an orange or grapefruit skin placed on the soil near to the plants. The beer trap is well worth trying and even weak beer has enough aroma to attract the slugs which then fall into the container to be poisoned by the minimal alcohol content and drowned. The beer should be discarded and replaced every couple of days for as long as it continues to trap the slugs and snails. An inexpensive method if you brew your own.

Slug pellets containing **Metaldehyde** can also be used to kill these pests if damage from them is widespread. Metaldehyde mixed with bran, when eaten by the slugs and snails, causes them to produce excessive amounts of slime. This in turn dehydrates them, greatly restricting their movement and eventually causing their death. This is not the perfect answer however as the slugs can recover from dehydration if rainfall follows ingestion of the pellets and also of course, the pellets will disintegrate if they get very wet.

Metaldehyde pellets are safe when used as directed, but care should be taken to ensure no spillages occur that could be accessible in quantity to pets or other birds and animals. Many people question why the pellets are blue. The answer is that blue is not a colour which mammals and birds normally associate with food and this lessens the likelihood of the pellets being eaten by anything other than the slugs and snails they are intended to kill.

It should be remembered that even the best control measures will never be perfect so it will always be a case of 'live and let live' with the slugs and snails we have failed to detect and destroy. We must not, and should not, expect to get rid of them all. Far better that a few are left for the blackbirds to feast upon.

Summary

- **Kill with beer traps wherever possible.**
- **Use Metaldehyde pellets if infestation is severe.**
- **If left uncontrolled damage is likely to be severe.**

Spider Mites greatly enlarged

Red Spider & Bryobia Mites

These mites, closely related to spiders, are a serious pest of warm greenhouses and in hot summers can attack certain plants outside in the garden. They are minute creatures, about 0.25 mm and not easily seen without the aid of a magnifying lens. The two most common species can cause serious damage to many plants, most often in the greenhouse or in the home, but also to plants outside, including many fruit trees and cane fruit.

Red Spider Mite

Being very small and living on the underside of the leaves, **red spider mites** are often undetected until the host plant begins to show the characteristic leaf symptoms of a mosaic pattern, fine mottling and sometimes 'bronzing' of the leaves. Fine webbing is spun by this mite, festooned on the leaves and stems of the plants being attacked.

Examination of the underside of affected leaves with a magnifying lens will reveal colonies of the mites feeding on the plant sap. Small, spherical white eggs are also usually visible in clusters around the feeding mites. These are likely to predominate alongside the main vein of the leaf but can occur elsewhere on the plant. In severe infestations plants can become very disfigured and weakened resulting, in some cases, in a complete loss of vigour and the eventual death of the plant.

Bryobia Mites

Symptoms of **bryobia mite** attack are similar to those of the red spider mite, infested plants showing leaf mottling, especially characteristic 'leaf bronzing', often followed by complete leaf fall after a month or so if the mites remain undetected.

Unlike the red spider mite reproduction is parthenogenetic and indeed males of this species are not known. Again unlike the red spider mite they do not produce webbing and because of this infestations are often unnoticed until the leaf damage is so severe that it becomes apparent something is seriously wrong.

A number of other mites can be troublesome in the garden including the **cyclamen** or **strawberry mite**, the **pear leaf blister mite**, and a number of **gall mites**, most notably the **blackcurrant gall mite**. This pest causes the condition known as 'big bud' in blackcurrants.

Mite Control

Bifenthrin, which is marketed in garden centres under a number of different brand names, is effective. This is also a useful general insecticide for aphids, whitefly etc and being a pyrethrin-based product it is reasonably safe to use. As ever, be sure to read the label thoroughly before use and follow the instructions to the letter.

A hot, dry atmosphere favours spider mite infestations especially in the protected conditions that exist within the greenhouse and in the home. Maintaining some humidity around the plants by misting them regularly will go a long way towards preventing a serious spider mite attack. Biological control is also possible using the predator **Phytoseiulus persimilis**. This is a slightly larger mite than the plant feeding red spider mite. This predator will consume the pest mite adults as well the immature young and will lay its eggs amongst the colonies of the pest. The eggs hatch when high greenhouse temperatures are maintained and the young predatory mites rapidly seek out their prey, eventually completely eradicating the pest. When this happens the predator dies out due to the lack of suitable food.

Summary

- **Some control of red spider and other mites can be achieved using Bifenthrin at the recommended high rate only.**
- **Biological control is very effective in the greenhouse using the predatory mite Phytoseiulus persimilis.**
- **To destroy the blackcurrant gall mite, spray the bushes with Bifenthrin.**
- **After spraying always remove and burn any of the infested buds showing the characteristic swelling known as 'big bud disease'.**

Eelworms - nematodes

Nematodes or **eelworms** are tiny creatures forming several groups. **Cyst eelworms**, of which the **potato cyst eelworm** is the most common, together with **free living eelworms,** are up to 1mm in size. Many species are parasitic, feeding on both plants and animals. Plants with poor growth, yet well fed and cared for and where no other obvious signs of pest or disease attack are evident, may be hosting a population of nematodes.

Stem eelworms and **root knot eelworms** are quite common though rarely correctly diagnosed unless analysed by a specialist laboratory. Commonly affected are narcissi bulbs, onions, broad beans, strawberries, parsnips, carrots, and other root crops. Symptoms vary from swollen roots, brittle leaves, brown staining and, with onions and narcissi, brown rings within the softened bulb.

The potato cyst nematode (PCN) is found where potatoes are grown on an infected site, where crop rotations have not been followed or where a previously clean site has been infected by the use of poor or 'home saved' seed potatoes. Always buy seed potatoes from a good supplier to prevent introducing PCN into your garden. Symptoms of PCN infestations include poor growth, distorted leaves and plants prone to wilting in dry weather. Sometimes the death of a plant occurs during the growing season and may not be noticed. If lifted many small yellow or white cysts may be found clinging to the roots. These cysts contain anything between 200 and 400 eggs. The eggs remain dormant, but still viable for up to five years, unknown and unseen. Many other plants can be grown on this soil with no ill effects, and with no inkling that there is a contamination beneath the soil. The dormancy is broken however once a potato or other solanum crop is planted. The normal chemical exudation from the new potato seed is sensed by the eggs and activates hatching leading to an infestation in the new crop. Infested plants can amount to 50% of the crop with a disastrous reduction in yield.

Potatoes and other solanum crops should not be planted in the same ground for a minimum period of 5 years. This long rotation, together with the use of certified seed, will ensure PCN does not infest clean garden soil and other pests and diseases will be reduced as a bonus.

Summary

- Carefully rotate crops.
- Always buy certified seed potatoes and be cautious when offered plants, tubers and rhizomes for the garden.
- If soil is infested potatoes or any other solanum family plant should not be planted for at least 5 years

Gardener's Friends

Insects and other arthropods

Probably at least 30 - 50% of all the insects we regularly see in our gardens are not only harmless but are in fact helpful in our fight against the insect pests.

Ladybirds

A number of beetles are carnivorous predators, the most well known of these and everyone's favourite is the **ladybird**. Many different species of ladybird live in the UK, as many as forty or so, with the 7 spot ladybird being perhaps the most common. All, with just one vegetarian exception, are predatory beetles eating enormously high numbers of pests such as aphids and other small insects. Ladybird larvae, which look a little like tiny, blue crocodiles with yellow spots, consume aphids at a phenomenal rate and compete with the adult beetle's fine

Ladybird larva

performance in despatching the pest. They should always be treated as welcome guests in the garden and encouraged in the excellent work they do. One small word of warning - although attractive the adult ladybird can also bite human flesh and will if it is in any way aggravated. It is sensible therefore to be careful if you are handling them.

Hoverflies

Well over 200 species of **hoverfly** occur in the UK and some, though not all by any means, are useful in the garden by assisting in the pollination of flowers and their larvae consuming large quantities of aphids. Many species, for their own protection, mimic the appearance and colour of honey bees and wasps, with one species being easily

Ladybird eating black aphids with ant tending the Aphids

Hoverfly

Green Lacewing

mistaken for a small bumble bee. All hoverflies are remarkably skilful fliers. Their hovering ability, and the incredible speed with which they can change their direction of flight is quite wonderful to watch. Thankfully, they don't sting.

Lacewings

Often entering our houses at night, having been lured in by the bright light, the **green lacewings** are most attractive insects. Large gold coloured eyes and their finely veined wings, together with their luminous pale green colour, single them out as being creatures that even the most 'anti-insect' human

Green Lacewing larva

can accept. They really are quite beautiful and one of nature's true works of art. As well as being attractive they are decidedly useful allies in the garden. Both the larvae and the adult flies are carnivorous, feasting on the dreaded aphid as well as other small insect pests.

Interestingly, gardens with mature, though not necessarily large trees seem to support the largest populations of both our common lacewings, the green and also the slightly smaller brown species.

Spiders & Mites

The spider family contains many species that are helpful in the garden but pride of place must be given to the **garden spider**. It can often be seen suspended in the middle of its web in the early morning before the warm sun has evaporated the dew. This particular spider is quite large and easily recognised by its heart-shaped abdomen and the distinct cross-shaped pattern on its back. It is rare to find this spider indoors as it is essentially a creature at home in the garden herbage and most gardens, even very small ones, support a number of individuals. The spider

63

diet consists of various flies and midges caught in the very elaborate and beautiful web. They are a most welcome addition to any garden, assisting in keeping pests down to reasonable numbers.

Not all **mites** are pests as some of the larger ones are carnivorous and, like spiders, feed on their smaller pest cousins. Differentiating between the two however is a difficult task and a specialist knowledge of mites is required. As a rough guide it is fairly safe to say that any mites living on the soil are likely to be useful predators whereas visible plant damage, as previously described, reveals the presence of the smaller pest mites.

Dragonflies

Useful and beautiful creatures, the dragonflies are most helpful to the gardener. Being insect eaters they can be seen where a stretch of water such as a pond is nearby, hawking up and down over the lawns and flower beds in a distinct and precise pattern, catching midges,

Banded demoiselle - male

mosquitoes, winged aphids and other small insects, on the wing.

Many different species can be seen, most of them vividly coloured, from the blue and green **damsel flies**, to the very large thicker bodied species, many equally colourful. All of them not only keep plant pests down but also reduce the number of pests that can physically attack the gardener and inflict painful bites.

Bumble Bee

Bees & Wasps

The bees, including the **honey bee**, the **bumble bee** and the **solitary bees**, are the flower pollinators par excellence. Although the females of these species can inflict painful stings this usually only occurs when the insect has been provoked in some way. It is unfortunate that often what we believe is kindly caring behaviour towards the bee can be misinterpreted as a provocation. A rather painful sting can follow.

All the bees feed their young on

Honey Bee

pollen and nectar from the flowers they visit and it is this foraging that assists pollination, the pollen having been transported on the legs and body of the bee.

A question we have all often asked is 'What possible use to the world is a **wasp**?' Actually, the common wasp really is very useful. Yes, they do have a painful sting, they do have a peculiarly erratic flight especially when near humans and yes, they can destroy fruit such as apples and pears if these have been in any way previously damaged by birds or by some other means. Furthermore, in the late summer, when the wasp is changing from a carnivorous diet to sweeter sugary foods, flower buds, such as roses, can be seriously damaged by their chewing of the emerging petals. On one occasion in mid-August and having been stung by a wasp the previous week, I watched, with considerable satisfaction I might add, an incongruous and bitter fight between two wasps trying to take possession of a single bud on one of my favourite roses, 'Fragrant cloud'. After much vicious battling one of them finally gave up and flew off to an adjoining bush, the other settling down to chew away at his favourite bud leaving behind a mass of fine, chewed frass, rather like tobacco dust.

Common Wasp

So what use are they in the order of things? Wasps are carnivorous insects for a large part of their lives, feeding themselves and their young on other insects including many pest species. They are also, from time to time, useful pollinators. At the end of summer however they turn to sweet things for their food when their normal meaty insect food is declining. As we all know it is at this time that they become most irritating and dangerous to us humans, seeking out our pots of jam, fruit etc and presenting a very real hazard to those who would picnic at this time of the year. They are, nonetheless, useful insects both as pollinators and destroyers of other garden pests.

Ichneumon Flies and Digger Wasps

These two families of insects are parasitic creatures. Both are valuable inhabitants of the garden as they play an unusual part in keeping pest numbers down.

The **ichneumon** in particular is a most useful predator of caterpillars, upon which it will settle. Using its ovipositor it pierces the caterpillar skin and lays its eggs inside the host. When the eggs hatch the small larvae set to work eating the inside of the caterpillar. By some quite remarkable intelligence, or perhaps genetic instinct, the parasite confines its eating at first to the non-vital organs within the

Potter Wasp dragging paralysed caterpillar to its nest

caterpillar body thereby keeping the caterpillar alive, though much weakened for as long as possible. Only on nearing maturity will the parasitic larvae consume the caterpillar's essential organs so ensuring the caterpillar's ultimate death.

The **digger wasps**, of which four species occur in this country, and the **potter wasp**, first paralyse their prey, usually a caterpillar, then carry it back to the wasp nest where the creature lays its eggs on the victim. Once the eggs have hatched, the larvae consume the paralysed caterpillar. Digger wasps and ichneumons are sometimes seen trapped inside our house windows, recognisable by their thin bodies with nipped waists and also by the distinct orange/brown colour of the two Ammophila species.

Centipedes

The **centipede** is a useful creature in the garden, attacking and eating many pest insects, small slugs and snails and their eggs. All centipedes are highly active and can run very quickly when disturbed or when searching for food. Female centipedes, in common with the earwig, are very caring and diligent towards their young, protecting them and shepherding them until they are able to look after themselves above ground.

The species most often seen in the garden is the orange/brown Lithobius forficatus, known as the common **garden centipede**. Another centipede, of the cryptops

Centipede (Cryptops)

family, is sometimes seen in the garden, especially near woodland. It is not as common as the garden centipede, is less brightly coloured and, to help us identify it, each of its body segments are of the same size, whereas the **common garden centipede** has wide and narrow segments which run alternately along the creature's back. All centipedes have one pair of legs per body segment, so they are unlikely to be confused with millipedes as these pests have two pairs of legs per segment and are far less highly coloured. The first pair of legs of the centipede are modified to catch and grip their prey and contain a venom to poison the unfortunate victim. The centipedes in this country are not dangerous to man but may cause slight discomfort to your skin if they bite you when handled. There are some centipedes in other parts of the world however which are much larger creatures, catching and eating frogs and even mice as part of their diet. Handling these larger centipedes may well result in a very nasty venomous bite which could be dangerous to children and those who are susceptible or allergic to the venom.

67

Garden Chemicals and Pest Control

At the present time many of the garden chemicals we have used over the past ten or more years have been withdrawn from public use. For reasons of safety and public health, directives have been issued within the European Community prohibiting the sale and use of certain products until further research on both their safety and efficacy has been completed. This is a very costly and time-consuming procedure and has resulted in the withdrawal of many very valuable products. There is no doubt that certain of these, if not used correctly and with the utmost care, can be a very considerable health hazard to the domestic user. Others, again if not used responsibly, are capable of causing serious and sometimes irreversible damage to the environment. Whilst regretting the loss of these products, which have served gardeners so well in the past, it is far better that we use products that carry minimal risk to those who use them whilst still achieving the pest control result required.

Chemical manufacturers throughout the world are working on new, better and safer products to use in our armoury against the ravages of pests. Not only safer for the gardener, but also more selective in their mode of operation, they reduce any potential harm to wildlife and the environment. Gardeners, as well as commercial growers, have a responsibility to be fully conversant with current legislation relating to the use of crop protection products and to use them strictly according to the manufacturers' instructions.

The safe use of Garden Chemicals

Always carefully read the label! It's there to protect you and the environment, and to make sure you achieve the results you are looking for.

- **Spray chemicals only when necessary.**

- **Avoid spraying in hot, bright sunlight when leaf damage occurs. Spray in early morning or early evening to protect beneficial insects such as bees and hover flies.**

- **Wear protective clothing if possible.**

- **Take care. Do not contaminate skin or clothing.**

- **If skin contamination occurs, wash off immediately.**

- **Do not breathe the spray mist.**

- **Do not eat, drink, or smoke, when handling or spraying chemicals.**

- **Always dispose of used containers safely.**

- **Do not contaminate ditches or watercourses.**

- **Store all chemicals under lock and key, where there is no access for children or family pets.**

- **Always wash hands and face after using chemicals, and wash any contaminated clothing.**

Chemical insecticides for garden use

All manufactured chemical insecticides are foreign substances to both our plants and ourselves. Most garden plants are tolerant of these products however, provided they are used correctly and in accordance with the label instructions, especially in regard to the quantities used. Insecticides may have varying modes of action. They can be contact insecticides, only effective if the pest is actually contaminated with the chemical. The spray residue may or may not persist on the sprayed plant. If it should persist it may control by contact any pests which arrive and get their feet wet after the spraying operation and also, if a vapour is present, it will deter other pests from settling on the plant.

Some of these products are designed to have a persistent residual activity and are a halfway house between contact and 'systemic' products.

The truly systemic products are those which enter the sap stream of the plant and are translocated in the vascular system to all aerial parts of the plant and, in some cases, movement to and through the plant roots. This effectively controls biting and sap sucking pests once they commence feeding.

Of these systemics some products have a short persistence while others have a much longer duration of activity. It is this latter more persistent group of insecticides which continue to give cause for concern.

In the case of edible crops of fruit and vegetables, including salads, the danger of taint and the possibility of toxic residues remaining in our food is very real. 'Harvest interval', the time that must elapse between spraying and picking, is much increased when systemic chemicals are used.

Although systemics are very effective in protecting the whole plant, sometimes for as long as 4 weeks, the persistence within the plant inevitably decreases if the plant is still growing strongly. It may then be necessary to boost the protection by applying a further spray at a later date.

A number of organo-phosphate insecticides, many of which are quite persistent and which have been in use for many years, have now been withdrawn on safety grounds. Some of much lower persistence are still available to commercial growers but even these are under threat of being banned. This follows the withdrawal from retail sale many years ago of insecticides from the extremely persistent and residual organo-chlorine group such as DDT, Dieldrin and Aldrin. The danger to our environment is that when these persistent chemicals enter the food chain, as well as killing insects, disastrously they also kill birds and mammals. This was highlighted with great effect some years ago in Rachel Carson's book *Silent Spring*.

We must be thankful that chemists throughout the world are looking for new, safer products for us to use in our gardens and no doubt each year we will see new molecules to replace those we have used in the past. Already there is a wide range of synthesised Pyrethroid insecticides available, relying on the discovery that the plant Pyrethrum (Chrysanthemum coccineum) contains an active natural insecticide. Synthesis by our chemists of this ingredient within the plant has led to many safer insecticides being available for our use and a number of these are listed.

All are contact killers with one or two also active as stomach poisons if they are ingested by the pest.

Because of the mainly contact action of these pyrethrins however good coverage of the targeted plant is essential. Harvest intervals after spraying varies with the product used but all the Pyrethrins have short or very short intervals between spraying and harvesting, in some cases as little as 24 hours.

Legislation on the use of garden chemicals is constantly changing. Always check with your product supplier that the product you wish to use is still approved for your particular purpose and the plant, or crop, on which you intend to use it.

Various pests can also be controlled by the use of fatty acids, soaps, and certain vegetable oils, with a number of different types and brand names on the market. Look out for these on garden centre shelves, as many new products are becoming available.

Approved Garden Insecticides

Pests	Trade Name	Active Ingredient	Mode
Aphids Whitefly Mealybug Scale insects Ants Woodlice Caterpillars and Flies Spider Mites	Various trade names	**Pyrethrins** **Bifenthrin** ***Permethrin** *Now cleared for use, as a dust only* ***Deltamethrin** *For commercial use only* ***Tetramethrin** *For commercial use only* ***Cypermethrin** *For commercial use only* **Bifenthrin only, using a high dose rate.**	Contact, with some by ingestion. Some also have a residual quality. Some are dusts, some are sprays.

Pests	Trade Name	Active Ingredient	Mode
Aphids Whitefly Mealybug Scale insects Vine weevil Spider mite Lily beetle and other beetles	Provado	**Neonicotinoids** **Imidacloprid**	Contact sytemic, and a compost drench, for containerised plants. For ornamentals, tomatoes, peppers and aubergines only. No other food crops.

Natural organic insecticides

Pests	Trade Name	Active Ingredient	Mode
Caterpillars and other pests	Derris Liquid and powder available	**Rotenone**	Contact but poor on aphids. Can be used as a dust or a spray.

71

Biological and other controls

Instead of using pesticides there are now many biological and other options available, some of which are listed below.

Some pests can be controlled using predators such as certain wasps, flies and beetles. Insect parasites and diseases are also used for pest control to avoid the long term effects of worldwide and sometimes indiscriminate chemical usage. The following biological organisms are available from specialist companies and are supplied with full instructions for use. Most are only suitable for use in the greenhouse or areas of protected cultivation.

The Pest	The Biological Control	Area of Use
Aphids	Ladybird – predator	Garden & greenhouse
	Aphelinus spp – parasite	Greenhouse
	Aphidius spp – parasite	Greenhouse
	Lacewing larvae – predator	Greenhouse
Whitefly	Encarsia formosa – parasite	Greenhouse
Mealybug	Cryptolaemus – predator	Greenhouse
Slugs & snails	Phasmarhabditis – nematode	Garden & greenhouse
Caterpillars	Caterpillar nematode	Garden & greenhouse
Red spider mite	Phytoseiulus – predator	Greenhouse
Vine weevil	Steinernema – nematode	Garden & greenhouse
Cockchafer & other chafer grubs	Heterorhabditis – nematode	Garden lawns & grassland
Leatherjacket	Steinernema – nematode	Lawns & grassland
Scale insects	Chilocorus nigritus – predator	Greenhouse
Sciarids	Fungus fly nematode	Garden, greenhouse and compost heap
Ants	Ant nematode	Lawns & grassland
Thrips	Amblyseius – predator	Greenhouse

It is worth taking care when selecting which variety of plant to grow. Many are now available which are not only disease-resistant, but also pest-resistant and where possible these varieties should be chosen. In the greenhouse yellow sticky traps catch flying pests. Of course these traps must always be removed before a flying biological control parasite is introduced.

Pheromone traps are available for various moths such as codling and pea moths. Separate pheromone lures are used for each type of moth, the lures using the scent of the female to attract and trap the male, ensuring that the females do not lay fertile eggs. In addition placing a grease band around the tree trunk throughout the winter will catch the moths as they climb up from the soil below.

A grease band can be placed around containers to deter insects such as ants and earwigs from reaching the plants and grease can be put round plant stems to prevent earwigs getting to the flowers.

Strawberry seed beetles can be caught by sinking several jam jars, half full of water, up to their rim into the ground within the strawberry bed.

Half a grapefruit or orange skin on the soil close to the plants makes a simple trap for slugs. This should be checked daily and the slugs removed. Alternatively a beer trap, made from a straight-sided container filled with beer and sunk to rim level in the soil, will attract slugs and snails.

Flowerpots placed upside down in the borders with a small gap left for them to enter will attract snails, which can then be removed from the pot in the morning.

Slugs and snails do not like moving over rough surfaces - a layer of grit around the plants will deter them.

A flowerpot filled with hay or straw will act as a trap for earwigs. The pot should be placed upturned on a bamboo cane at the height of the flowers, checked in the evening and any earwigs removed.

To protect against carrot fly a barrier made from fine mesh fixed to a frame and placed around the bed will prevent the low-flying insects reaching the crop. Horticultural fleece can also be placed over the carrot crop until the plants become too large.

Collars placed around individual brassica plants stop cabbage root flies reaching the soil to lay their eggs.

Companion plantings can be used, such as planting nasturtiums within tomato crops to deter whitefly and, perhaps more widely known and used, planting marigolds within a crop to deter a whole range of pests. For plants highly attractive to aphids, some gardeners believe that growing onions alongside them reduces the risk of severe infestations. I do not know whether this works but personally I prefer to stick to a good crop rotation in my vegetable garden which in itself prevents excessive pest build-up, as well as minimising the risk of disease build-up and the likelihood of nutrient depletion.

Garden Chemical Manufacturers & Suppliers

Bayer Crop Science Ltd
0845 3454100
www.bayergarden.co.uk

Certis UK
01980 676500
www.certiseurope.co.uk

Gem Gardening
01254 356600
www.gemgardening.co.uk

The Scotts Miracle-Gro Company
08705 301010
www.lovethegarden.com

William Sinclair Horticulture Ltd
01522 537561
www.william-sinclair.co.uk

Syngenta Crop Protection UK Ltd
0800 1696058
www.syngenta.co.uk

Vitax Ltd
01530 510060
www.vitax.co.uk

Westland Horticulture Ltd
02887 727500
www.gardenhealth.com

Biological Pest Control Suppliers

Agralan Ltd
01285 860015
www.agralan.co.uk

Biowise
01798 867574
www.biowise-biocontrol.co.uk

Defenders Ltd
01233 813121
www.defenders.co.uk

Garden Organic (Henry Doubleday Research Association)
02476 303517
www.gardenorganic.co.uk

Green Gardener
01603 715096
www.greengardener.co.uk

Just Green
01621 785088
www.just-green.com

Scarletts Plant Care
01206 242533
www.scarletts.co.uk

Other Useful Contacts

Crop Protection Association
www.garden-care.org.uk

Department of Environment, Food and Rural Affairs (DEFRA)
020 7238 6000
www.defra.gov.uk

Garden Centre Association
0118 932 3360
www.gca.org.uk

GardenWorld
www.gardenworld.co.uk

Royal Horticultural Society
0845 260 5000
www.rhs.org.uk

January	Slugs and snails active in mild conditions. When digging look out for leatherjacket, wireworms and cockchafer grubs.
February	Slugs and snails, millipedes, and other soil pests. In mild conditions aphids may appear, especially in sheltered areas.
March	Woodlice active in mild conditions. Flea beetles can attack early sown crops. When sowing or planting look out for all soil pests.
April	Early aphid attacks, cabbage root fly symptoms appear. Fruit beetles, weevils and spider mites may be active.
May	Aphids, whiteflies, capsids, froghoppers, apple and pear suckers, scale insects, thrips, sawflies and lily beetles are all active.
June	Caterpillars of butterflies and moths, together with all pests active in May. Ants may swarm.
July	Look out especially for cabbage white butterfly, eggs and caterpillars. Ants, aphids and whitefly are abundant in hot periods.
August	All the July pests are still in evidence, and may include new infestations of spider mites. Wasps are plentiful, persistent, and now change to feeding on a sweet diet.
September	Aphids and whiteflies persist. Possibly some late caterpillars.
October	If mild weather occurs aphids can be in evidence. Slugs and snails are also active.
November	All soil pests, slugs and snails.
December	Soil pests, slugs and snails. In the greenhouse aphids and whiteflies may still persist.

The above calendar is obviously only a rough guide to pest appearances, as each year, weather patterns will vary, both in timing and geographical location. So also, the seasonal occurrence of pests will always change, and often surprise us. Good gardeners will therefore watch for pests throughout the year.

Flower damage

Flowers with missing or damaged petals	**Earwigs & capsids**
Lily and some polygonum flowers shredded with infestation of larval grubs	**Lily beetle**
Colonies of whitish, waxy small insects clustered around opening flower buds of house plants and particularly in the greenhouse	**Mealybugs**
Flower petals of many plants eaten, with characteristic silvery slime left on the plant and surrounding soil or Compost	**Slugs & snails**
Damage to buds and flowers, together with silvery lines, mottling and disfigured leaves, of gladioli and many other plants including iris and roses	**Thrips**

Stem damage

Sooty black mould and insects clustered on stems, particularly in the greenhouse	**Aphids, whiteflies**
Blobs of frothy spit on stems, with many plants including grasses affected	**Froghoppers**
Small, hard, brown or yellow scales on stems of ornamental plants, particularly in the greenhouse	**Scale insects**
Colonies of whitish, waxy, small insects around the stems of house plants and in the greenhouse	**Mealybugs**
Lilies infested with larval grubs on stems and leaves which are covered in black slime	**Lily beetle**
Disfigured stems of nasturtiums and cabbages with many grubs and excreta usually present	**Caterpillars**
Stems of young seedlings in seed boxes severed	**Woodlice, slugs & snails**

Leaf damage

Sooty black mould disfiguring leaves of many plants, particularly in greenhouses but also outside, as well as on many trees	**Aphids, whiteflies**

Small, neat holes on many leaves of young plants, particularly brassicas and some ornamentals	**Flea beetles**
Mosaic mottling on upper surface of leaves, with leaves often bronzing, and webbing sometimes but not always apparent	**Spider mites**
Leaf holes with ragged edges (larger than flea beetle damage) on ornamentals and fruit trees	**Capsids**
Large areas of leaf eaten, perhaps skeletalised, on brassicas and nasturtiums. Many grubs and excreta usually present	**Caterpillars**
White mottling on upper surface of leaves of roses, shrubs, trees, greenhouse tomatoes, houseplants, cane fruit and ornamental plants	**Leaf hoppers**
Lily leaves, and some polygonums, shredded with infestation of larval grubs on leaves and stems, all covered in black slime	**Lily beetle**
Small, hard, brown or yellow scales on underside of leaves. Fouling of older foliage, prevalent on fruit trees, ornamental plants and shrubs, especially in the greenhouse	**Scale insects**
Colonies of whitish, waxy, small insects clustered around the leaf axils and stems of house plants, particularly in the greenhouse	**Mealybugs**
Leaf margins with irregular portions eaten away, particularly on plants or trees growing against a wall	**Woodlice**
Rose leaves tightly rolled up into a cylinder, with larvae eating inside the rolled leaf	**Leaf-rolling sawfly**
Silvery lines, mottling and disfigured leaves of gladioli, some distortion may also be present. Also damage to leaves, buds and flowers of many other plants including peas, onions, iris and roses	**Thrips**
Leaves of many plants eaten, with characteristic silvery slime left on the plant and on the surrounding soil or compost	**Slugs & snails**
Solomon's seal with severe leaf shredding by grey, caterpillar-like maggots	**Solomon's seal sawfly larvae**

Silken webs, drawing the edges of leaves together, and harbouring a grub inside	**Tortrix moth caterpillar**
Very small holes in the ground level leaves of many plants, particularly house plants and seedling plants in the greenhouse. Flea-like insects may be present	**Springtails**
Shredded leaves of dahlias, chrysanthemums, zinnias and other flowering plants	**Earwigs**
Scalloped leaf margins to broad beans and peas	**Pea & bean weevil**
Celery leaves with blotches of dead leaf tissue	**Celery fly**
Carrot leaves becoming a bronze colour	**Aphids, but may be carrot fly**
Small, neat holes on many leaves of young plants, particularly brassica plants including radish, swedes, turnips and cabbages and some ornamentals	**Flea beetles**

Fruit damage

Apples and pears with damaged skins and cracks on the surface	**Capsids**
Maggots inside cut apples, sometimes with an exit hole showing on the skin surface	**Codling moth**
Damaged apple skins, with cavities, and premature fruit fall	**Apple sawfly**
Gooseberry bushes with severe defoliation	**Gooseberry sawfly, magpie moth**
Cane fruit with mottled upper surface of leaves	**Leafhoppers**
Pear fruitlets failing to develop, turning black and falling prematurely	**Pear midge**
Severe damage to leaves of pear trees, black maggots visible on leaves	**Pear tree slugworm**
Plums falling prematurely, with caterpillars inside fruit	**Plum moth**
Raspberries with small maggots eating the fruit	**Raspberry beetle**

Damaged strawberry fruit	**Slugs, strawberry seed beetle, damage from blackbirds**
Strawberry plants with brittle leaves and swollen roots	**Eelworms**
Leaf holes with ragged edges on fruit trees	**Capsids**

Vegetable damage

Celery leaves with blotches of dead leaf tissue	**Celery fly**
Carrot foliage becoming a bronze colour	**Aphids, carrot fly**
Damage to leaves and stems of asparagus	**Asparagus beetle**
Scalloped leaf margins to broad beans and peas	**Pea & bean weevil**
Large areas of leaf eaten, perhaps skeletalised with cabbages and other brassicas. Many grubs and excreta usually present	**Caterpillars**
Potatoes showing poor growth, wilting and distorted foliage. Small white and yellow cysts on the roots	**Potato cyst eelworm**
White mottling on upper surface of leaves of greenhouse tomatoes	**Leaf hoppers**
Fruit trees with small, hard, brown or yellow scales on underside of leaves, fouling of older foliage	**Scale insects**
Damage to leaves of peas and onions	**Thrips**
Leaves of many vegetable plants eaten, with characteristic silvery slime left on the plant and on the surrounding soil or compost	**Slugs & snails**
Vegetable seedlings with stems severed at soil level	**Cutworms**
Potatoes and other tubers with holes and internal damage	**Slugs**
Cabbages and other brassicas wilting and with pink or purple discolouration	**Cabbage root fly**
Damaged roots and tubers, particularly on root crops	**Chafer grubs, leatherjackets, keeled slugs**

79

Onions having brown rings within the bulb	**Eelworms**
Root crops with swollen roots and brittle leaves	**Eelworms**
Brown staining on broad beans	**Eelworms**
Small holes in potato tubers, with internal damage	**Millipedes**
Small, neat holes on many leaves of young plants, particularly brassica plants including radish, swedes, turnips and cabbages	**Flea beetles**
White maggots, 5 - 8 mm long, in leaves, stems and bulbs of onions, shallots and leeks	**Onion fly**
Tough skinned white or yellow larvae, thin but up to 25 mm long, living in soil and attacking potatoes and many other vegetables. Small holes 2 – 3 mm in diameter are made in potatoes and other tubers and bulbs. These holes are often enlarged by millipedes and slugs to gain access to the internal flesh	**Wireworm**
Stunted growth of young greenhouse tomato plants, especially in calcareous soils	**Symphylids**
Bright red larvae on potato and other solanums	**Colorado beetle**

Underground damage to Roots, Bulbs and Tubers

Tough skinned white, or yellow larvae, thin, but up to 25 mm long, living in soil, and attacking potatoes as well as many other vegetables and ornamental plants. Small holes 2 - 3mm in diameter are made in potatoes and other tubers and bulbs. These holes are often enlarged by millipedes and slugs to gain access to the internal flesh	**Wireworm**
Potatoes, other tubers and bulbs, with holes and internal damage	**Slugs**
Stunted growth of young tomato plants, growing in the greenhouse, especially in calcareous soils	**Symphylids**
Carrot foliage becoming bronzed	**Carrot fly**

Damaged roots and tubers, particularly on root crops, dahlias etc, following grass, but all plants susceptible to root damage and wilting	**Chafer grubs, leatherjackets, keeled slugs**
Onions and narcissi having brown rings within the bulb. Swollen roots and brittle leaves of other root crops	**Eelworms**
Small holes in potato tubers, bulbs, corms and rhizomes, with internal damage	**Millipedes**
Potatoes showing poor growth, wilting, and distorted foliage. Small white and yellow cysts on the roots	**Potato cyst eelworm**
Cabbages and other brassicas, wilting, and with pink or purple discolouration	**Cabbage root fly**
Pot plants showing stunted growth, and symptoms of wilting	**Vine weevil**
White maggots 5 – 8 mm long in leaves, stems and bulbs of onions, shallots and leeks	**Onion fly**

English	Latin
Angle shades moth	Phlogophora meticulosa
Apple capsid	Plesiocoris rugicollis
Apple sucker	Psylla mali
Asparagus beetle	Crioceris asparagi
Bay laurel sucker	Trioza alacris
Black ant	Lasius niger
Black bean aphid	Aphis fabae
Black keeled slug	Milax budapestensis
Black millipede	Tachypodiolus niger
Black slug	Arion ater
Blackcurrant gall	Cecidophyopsis ribis
Bryobia mites	Bryobia spp
Bumble bee	Bombus agrorum
Cabbage root fly	Delia brassicae
Cabbage whitefly	Aleyrodes proletella
Carrot fly	Psila rosae
Celery fly	Euleia heracle
Centipede	Lithobius variegates
Click beetle - wireworm	Dascillus cervinus
Cockchafer	Melolontha melolontha
Codling moth	Cydia pomonella
Colorado beetle	Leptinotarsa decemlineata
Common cutworm	Noctua pronuba
Common green capsid	Calocoris norvegicus
Common wasp	Vespula vulgaris
Crane Fly - leatherjacket	Tipula paludosa
Cyclamen - strawberry mite	Tarsonemus pallidus
Damsel fly	Caloptreyx splendens
Digger wasp	Ammophila sabulosa
Earwig	Forficula auricularia
Flat millipede	Brachydesmus superus
Flea beetle	Phyllotreta undulata
Froghopper	Philaenus spumarius
Garden snail	Helix aspera

English	Latin
Garden spider	Araneus diadematus
Glasshouse & potato aphid	Aulacorthum solani
Glasshouse thrip	Heliothrips haemorrhoidalis
Goat moth	Cossus cossus
Gooseberry sawfly	Nematus ribesii
Green lacewing	Chrysopa carnea
Grey field slug	Derocera reticulatum

Hawk moth	Deilephila elpenor
Honey bee	Apis mellifera
Hoverfly	Syrphus ribesii

Ladybird	Coccinella septempunctata
Large white butterfly	Pieris brassicae
Leaf rolling sawfly	Blennocampa pusilla
Leafhopper	Cercophid
Lily beetle	Lilioceris lilii

Magpie moth	Abraxus grosslariata
Mealy bug	Cryptolaemus montouzieri

Onion fly	Delia antiqua
Onion thrip	Thrips tabaci

Pea & bean weevil	Sitona lineatus
Pea moth	Cydia nigricana
Pear leaf blister mite	Eriophyes pyri
Pear midge	Contarinia pyrivora
Pear sucker	Psylla pyricola
Pear tree sawfly	Caliroa cerasi
Plum aphid	Brachycaudas helichrysi
Potato cyst eelworm	Globodera rostochiensis
Potter wasp	Eumenes pedunculatus
Puss moth	Cerura vinula

Raspberry beetle	Byturus tomentosus
Red ant	Myrmica ruginoides
Red spider mite	Acarina
Rose aphid	Macrosiphum rosae
Rose thrip	Thrips fuscipennis

Scale insect	Coccus hesperidum
Sciarid fly	Sciarid spp
Silver y moth	Autographa gamma

English	Latin
Small white butterfly	Pieris rapae
Solitary bee	Megachile centuncularis
Solomon's seal sawfly	Phymatocera ribesii
Spotted snake millipede	Blaniulus guttulatus
Springtail	Orchesella spp
Strawberry seed beetle	Harpalus rufipes
Swift moth	Hepialus lupulinus
Symphylid	Scutigerella immaculata
Thrip, gladiolus	Thrips simplex
Turnip Cutworm	Agrotis segetum
Vapourer moth	Orgyia antiqua
Vine Weevil	Otiorhynchus sulcatus
Whitefly	Trialeurodes vaporariorum
Wood wasp	Urocerus gigas
Woodlouse	Oniscus asellus

Latin	English
Abraxus grossulariata	Magpie moth
Acarina	Red spider mite
Agrotis segetum	Turnip cutworm
Aleyrodes proletella	Cabbage whitefly
Ammophila sabulosa	Digger wasp
Aphis fabae	Black bean aphid
Apis mellifera	Honey bee
Araneus diadematus	Garden spider
Arion ater	Black slug
Aulacorthum solani	Glasshouse & potato aphid
Autographa gamma	Silver y moth
Blaniulus guttulatus	Spotted snake millipede
Blennocampa pusilla	Leaf rolling sawfly
Bombus agrorum	Bumble bee
Brachycaudas helichrysi	Plum aphid
Brachydesmus superus	Flat millipede
Bryobia spp	Bryobia mites
Byturus tomentosus	Raspberry beetle
Caliroa cerasi	Pear tree sawfly

Latin	English
Calocoris norvegicus	Common green capsid
Cecidophyopsis ribis	Blackcurrant gall mite
Cercophid	Leafhopper
Cerura vinula	Puss moth
Chrysopa carnea	Green lacewing
Coccinella septempunctata	Ladybird
Coccus hesperidum	Scale insect
Contarinia pyrivora	Pear midge
Cossus cossus	Goat moth
Crioceris asparagi	Asparagus beetle
Cryptolaemus montouzieri	Mealybug
Cydia nigricana	Pea moth
Cydia pomonella	Codling moth
Dascillus cervinus	Click beetle - wireworm
Deilephila elpenor	Hawk moth
Delia antiqua	Onion fly
Delia brassicae	Cabbage root fly
Derocera reticulatum	Grey field slug
Eriophyes pyri	Pear leaf blister mite
Euleia heracle	Celery fly
Eumenes pedunculatus	Potter wasp
Forficula auricularia	Earwig
Globodera rostochiensis	Potato cyst eelworm
Harpalus rufipes	Strawberry seed beetle
Heliothrips haemorrhoidalis	Glasshouse thrip
Helix aspera	Garden snail
Hepialus lupulinus	Swift moth
Lasius niger	Black ant
Leptinotarsa decemlineata	Colorado beetle
Lilioceris lilii	Lily beetle
Lithobius variegates	centipede
Macrosiphum rosae	Rose aphid
Megachile centuncularis	Solitary bee

Latin	English
Melolontha melolontha	Cockchafer
Milax budapestensis	Black keeled slug
Myrmica ruginoides	Red ant
Nematus ribesii	Gooseberry sawfly
Noctua pronuba	Common cutworm
Oniscus asellus	Woodlouse
Orchesella spp	Springtail
Orgyia antiqua	Vapourer moth
Otiorhynchus sulcatus	Vine weevil
Philaenus spumarius	Froghopper
Phlogophora meticulosa	Angle shades moth
Phyllotreta undulata	Flea beetle
Phymatocera ribesii	Solomon's seal sawfly
Pieris brassicae	Large white butterfly
Pieris rapae	Small white butterfly
Plesiocoris rugicollis	Apple capsid
Psila rosae	Carrot fly
Psylla mali	Apple sucker
Psylla pyricola	Pear sucker
Sciarid spp	Sciarid fly
Scutigerella immaculata	Symphylid
Sitona lineatus	Pea & bean weevil
Syrphus ribesii	Hoverfly
Tachypodiolus niger	Black millipede
Tarsonemus pallidus	Cyclamen - strawberry mite
Thrips fuscipennis	Rose thrip
Thrips simpex	Thrip, gladiolus
Thrips tabaci	Onion thrip
Tipula paludosa	Crane fly - leatherjacket
Trialeurodes vaporariorum	Whitefly
Trioza alacris	Bay laurel sucker
Urocerus gigas	Wood wasp
Vespula vulgaris	Common wasp

Glossary

Brassicas	Members of the cabbage family, brussels sprouts, cauliflowers, broccoli, turnips etc.
Cuticle	The cutin surface of leaves, often waxy, as in peas, beans, and cabbages.
Diptera	Flies, having one pair of wings only.
Elytra	The hardened forewings of beetles, which cover and protect the rear wings.
Hermaphrodite	Having both male and female reproductive organs.
Honeydew	The surplus sugary fluid excreted by sap sucking insects, such as aphids and whiteflies.
Imago	An adult insect.
Larva	The young, immature insect, very different from the adult, such as fly maggots, caterpillars etc. All larvae must pupate before reaching the adult stage.
Metamorphosis	The process of changing from larva to adult.
Nymph	The young of certain insects such as whiteflies and aphids, which undergo only a partial metamorphosis, and pupation. Nymphs are usually similar to the adult insect.

Ovipositor   The egg-laying organ of the female insect.

Parthenogenesis   The ability to reproduce without fertilisation from the male insect.

Photosynthesis   The manufacture of sugars within the leaf. The chlorophyll in the leaf utilising sunlight, carbon dioxide and water, to produce sugars, and release oxygen into the atmosphere.

Prolegs   The false legs towards the rear of the caterpillar body.

Pupation   The third stage of metamorphosis, where the larva turns into a pupa. The pupa is usually immobile, and has ceased feeding, before emerging as an adult.

Residual   A term used for a crop protection product, including insecticides, weedkillers, and fungicides, that remains active on the leaf or soil surface for a limited period after its application.

Soil drench   A product applied in solution to soil or compost, giving an insecticidal or fungicidal effect within the growing medium.

Sooty moulds   Fungal moulds, Cladosporium spp, colonising the leaf surface and living on excreted honeydew.

Systemic   Products which permeate into the sap stream, thereby translocating to all parts of the growing plant.

Viviparous   Giving birth to live young, as distinct from laying or shedding eggs.

Index

NOTES